BUDGETING in 90

For a complete list of Management Books 2000 titles,
visit our web-site on http://www.mb2000.com

The original idea for the 'In Ninety Minutes' series was presented to the publishers by Graham Willmott, author of 'Forget Debt in Ninety Minutes'. Thanks are due to him for suggesting what has become a major series to help business people, entrepreneurs, managers, supervisors and others to greatly improve their personal performance, after just a short period of study.

Other titles in the 'in Ninety Minutes' series are:

Forget Debt in 90 Minutes
Understand Accounts in 90 Minutes
Working Together in 90 Minutes
25 Management Techniques in 90 Minutes
Supply Chain in 90 Minutes
Practical Negotiating in 90 Minutes
Faster Promotion in 90 Minutes
Find That Job in 90 Minutes
Become a Meeting Anarchist in 90 Minutes
Telling People in 90 Minutes
Strengths Coaching in 90 Minutes
Perfect CVs in 90 Minutes
Networking in 90 Minutes
Payroll in 90 Minutes
... other titles will be added

The series editor is James Alexander

Submissions of possible titles for this series or for management books in general will be welcome. MB2000 are always keen to discuss possible new works that might be added to their extensive list of books for people who mean business.

A simple but comprehensive approach to careful financial planning and getting those figures right

Sidney Callis

For Bim, with love ... always

First published in 2006 by Management Books 2000 Ltd
Forge House, Limes Road
Kemble, Cirencester
Gloucestershire, GL7 6AD, UK
Tel: 0044 (0) 1285 771441
Fax: 0044 (0) 1285 771055
E-mail: info@mb2000.com
Web: www.mb2000.com

Printed and bound in Great Britain by 4edge Ltd, Hockley. www.4edge.co.uk

British Library Cataloguing in Publication Data is available

ISBN 1-85252-509-6

Contents

Budgeting
What It Is and How To Do It

Introduction

Budgeting is the one function of management which many managers dread. 'It takes too much time.' 'It's meaningless, it's just an accounting exercise.' 'It is imposed from the top, we don't get a say about it!' These and many other comments are typical of how budgets are regarded by a great many managers. But budgeting is important, and it is important that it is done well. Because the budget is the most effective control tool for the success of any business, no matter how big or how small.

It is notorious that little training is ever provided for management; there is plenty of theory and lots of books. But generally the practical aspect of everyday hands-on running of the business – and that includes budgeting – is expected to be picked up as it goes along.

This book, written in straightforward, non-accountants' language, is designed to give anyone engaged in business, at any level, a clear understanding of what a budget is, how to compile it and how to use it. Our overall objectives are to introduce people to the skills needed for budgeting, to enhance existing skills, and to provide direction for them to function as effective members of a budgeting team.

Unfortunately, the process of putting a budget together is often dominated by the accountants. But budgeting isn't just dealing with figures; to do it well needs a lot of thought about the business.

- What business are we in?
- What assets (in the broadest sense) do we have?
- Where are we going and where do we want to be – what are our objectives?

Also it really needs cooperation and genuine involvement. Everyone in the business, from top to bottom, who is responsible for getting money in – sales – or spending money in any way associated with the activity of the business, needs to take part.

There is, it must be admitted, rather a lot to deal with and, although there is some accounting stuff, it is not rocket science! All the reader needs is a modicum of common sense, so as to apply the principles of budgeting that are described in the chapters that follow.

Chapter 1: Budgeting and Planning

- establishes what budgeting is about and the process.

Chapter 2: Budget Techniques

- sets out the ideas of responsibility accounting and the budget as an operating plan for the business.

Chapter 3: Budget Control Systems

- here we look at using the budget as the control mechanism for running the business effectively.

Chapter 4: Specific Budgeting Items

- deals with the building of the budget from its various components.

Chapter 5: Forecasting

- looks at the essential precursor to budgeting proper.

Chapter 6: Administering the Budget Programme

- here we have a detailed examination of how the whole budgeting processes is managed.

Chapter 7: Zero Base Budgeting

- this gives a brief overview of the system which shakes up traditional methods.

Chapter 8: The Budget of a Business

- a rapid revision of the whole process.

Finally, a note on style – it is obvious that we are equally male or female. We have tried to avoid the frequent use of 'he or she', which is rather clumsy. If you see a 'he' on its own, it also means 'she' on its own. Please imagine the opposite gender, because we are all endeavouring to do a good budgeting job.

1

Budgeting and Planning

1.1 The Budget, an essential element of the corporate plan

1.1.1 Introduction

Resources are relatively scarce. Management is concerned with the effective use of the resources available, to fulfil the function of the business. In any business, costs must be controlled if planned profits are to be realised year after year. The budget is about guiding the internal operations of the business to produce satisfactory profits at the lowest cost.

The budget is thus an integral part, and often the main expression, of the corporate planning process of a Company. There are several aspects to this process:

- There must be a formal management structure to support a responsibility accounting budget.
- A responsibility accounting process means that each executive is accountable for achieving the budget, as part of the overall corporate development plan.
- The responsibility budget needs a budgetary planning and control system.

This is the keystone of the corporate planning process. It is concerned with detailed planning and control in the short term.

The control systems must also be closely integrated with the company's long-term plans.

There are four aspects of the control process:

1. to **develop plans** to achieve objectives
2. to **communicate information** about proposed plans
3. to **motivate people** to accomplish the plans
4. to **report performance**.

Control is not a word that sounds pleasant to managers, but it is not concerned with the correction of past mistakes. Control is concerned with the direction of current and future activities, to ensure that management plans happen. Control means the ability to make decisions based on relevant information. This leads to plans and actions that improve the usage of the productive assets and services available to management.

Plans for, and the results of, operations need to be expressed in people terms, not as abstract concepts, because:

- people, rather than analyses or reports, control operations
- to do their jobs effectively, people need facts
- supplying the facts for control is an important budgeting function.

1.1.2 Responsibility areas defined

The relationship between the formal structure of a company – the organisation chart and the areas of responsibility is shown graphically in the following diagram.

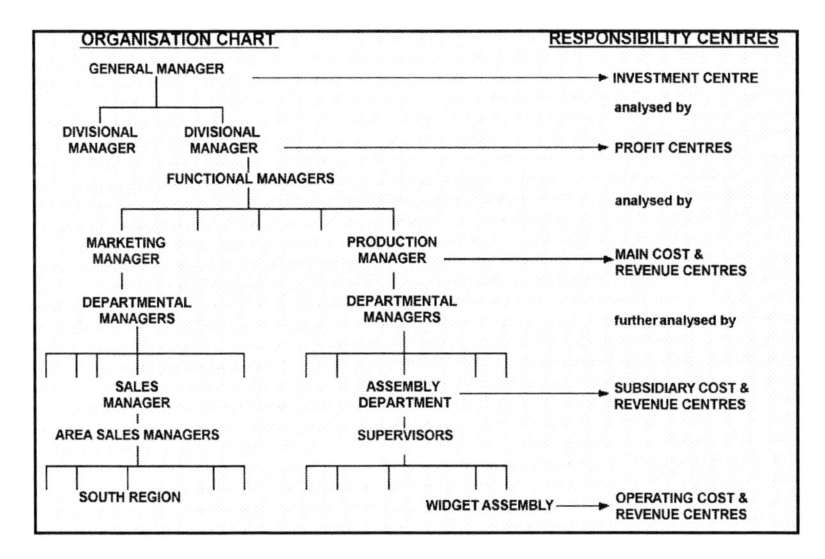

Relationship between organisation chart and responsibility centres

The people areas represent the various control centres within an organisation. Four possible types of responsibility centres can be defined in most companies; investment centres, profit centres, cost centres and revenue centres.

- The Manager of an investment centre is responsible for costs, revenues and assets employed, (the General Manager).
- Costs and revenues, but not investments, are controlled by the Manager of a profit centre, such as a product division, (for example, a marketing director).
- Cost centres are typified by a production department (for example, a factory or a functional area such as transport).
- Revenue centres (and cost centres) are found, for example, in a marketing department where a Sales Manager generates sales revenue as well as incurring expenses.

To provide effective control information to the decision-takers in an organisation, an accounting system which produces information analysed by responsibility centres is required. This is **responsibility accounting.**

The concept of responsibility accounting is the heart of budgetary planning and control. It is the essential management tool for planning, coordinating and controlling the activities of a business.

1.2 Management structure and the reporting network

The diagram opposite details the process to be followed and the diverse components to be dealt with in compiling a comprehensive budget for a business. We will explain all these elements in the following chapters.

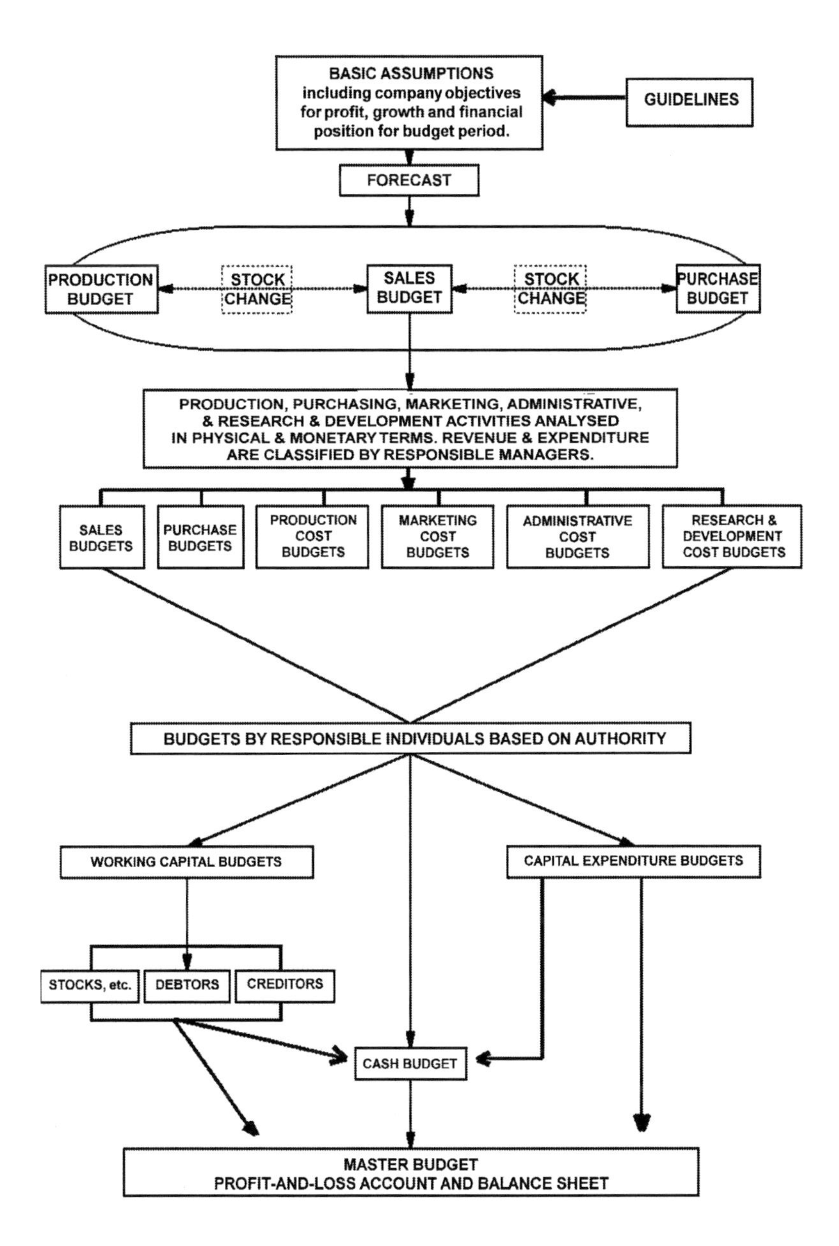

The components of a budget

1.2.1 How the reporting structures develop

Most organisations are not designed, they grow. But not all organisations adapt equally well to the environment in which they grow. To survive, an organisation needs to be fit.

For survival and for continual growth and development, organisations have to know what they want to be, before trying to become ... whatever it is. An organisation needs objectives. Analysis is the starting point for determining objectives and improvement and for planned change.

When a business starts, the objectives are usually quite clear – survive, make money. As it grows, these objectives are realised and other ideas are developed. These may conflict, so a coherent structure allocating formal responsibilities and harmonising objectives is needed. The typical mechanism is the organisation chart. This links the varying roles within the organisation to their functional operation. It is essential to keep the organisation chart 'live', so that it reflects the current structure and responsibilities in the Company.

These are determined by the size of the organisation, the people within the organisation, the market, its technology and the way it is developing. The organisation structure must fit in with the needs of responsibility accounting and budgetary control.

There are various designs to show management and reporting structures. The traditional 'family tree' is most favoured. This has advantages and disadvantages; but there are other innovative ways of displaying management relationships. Certain pressures have to be reconciled. The principle of: 'As simple as you can, as complex as you must' relates to the pressures of uniformity and diversity.

i. Uniformity

Uniformity implies standardisation with common procedures which are centrally administered. Uniformity is characteristic of the steady-state; a mature organisation which may be decaying, where cultural adherence to rules will predominate.

The pressures for uniformity include:

- **Cheapness** – training in standard procedures is easier and cheaper. There are economies of scale in most standardised operations.

- **Interchangeability** – many operations use common procedures. Interactions within the organisation can be carried out using standard procedures.

- **Control of process** – some organisations need to monitor their on-going operations rather than the results. Hence the need for uniformity of method.

- **Standard product** – organisations may need uniformity of output from various sources, e.g. standardised reporting formats.

- **Specialisation** – uniformity in the organisation will ensure a competence core. It is too costly to employ specialists.

- **Central control** – standardisation allows regular provision of critical information. Monitoring of the business and intervention is thus possible should it be needed. The requirement for central control can well be a desire for security by senior management rather than a need imposed by the situation.

ii. Diversity

Diversity is associated with complexity of structure.

Pressures in any organisation will make for diversity. These include:

- **Regional** – an organisation may operate in more than one geographical area. These will be defined as needed.

- **Market** – markets can be defined in regional terms, in socio-economic terms, by end-use, by customer activity or even by their social habits. Market categories and the degree to which they differ are important.

- **Product** – can the mix of outputs all be treated as one. Does each product have its own peculiarities in terms of market, image, need for servicing, quality, etc. The degree of difference matters.

- **Technological** – low tech permits wider ranges of expertise and shorter learning times. High tech is more pressing for diversity.

- **Goals** – does the organisation have one set of goals or do the goals vary? Does the variety matter? Internal diversity is common, when the market environment or the technology is rapidly changing.

- **Identity** – people find it easier to identify with smaller groups than with large organisations. Smaller groupings make it easier to identify with varied activities, rather than just one.

- **Decentralised control** – managers remote from the centre feel a need to have more control over their resources. Isolated groups try to get control redistribution.

- **Experiment** – the future cannot be systematically planned. There is growing respectability for more free-forms types of structure.

iii. Implications

Organisations seek to limit diversity and reduce uncertainty. Nevertheless they are affected by both uniformity and diversity. They prefer uniformity, which is predictable and efficient. The status quo cannot be the way forward. If organisations do not change, they will be overtaken by the competition.

The pressures of uniformity and diversity are an effective control element in any business. The organisation structure and reporting network needs to be stable, so that valid comparisons can be made year by year. The budgetary control system relies on uniformity, but must be aware of the possibilities of diversity so that the business can develop in a challenging environment.

To sum up:

- ➔ The budget is an essential element of the corporate plan for any business.
- ➔ The budget is the control mechanism of the business, not only to correct mistakes, but to guide operations towards the planned objective.
- ➔ People are involved in the running of a business; budget design and reporting must provide them with information to do their jobs.
- ➔ The management structure and reporting network must be integrated to provide information plus control.
- ➔ There are pressures to maintain uniformity, and to create diversity in reporting structure. Both have advantages and disadvantages depending on the stage of development of the business.
- ➔ A definition:

> **Budgeting is the preparation of a detailed operating plan which will meet or improve upon the profit objective by providing control.**

2

Budget Techniques and Types of Budget

2.1 Responsibility accounting

Budgets should be prepared by the individuals who will be responsible for achieving them. This ensures that full use is made of the knowledge of the people who know most about the detail. It also means that managers and their subordinates are committed to, and regard their budget as their intention.

The more 'grass roots' level the budgeting process starts from, the better chance there will be of getting realistic results. With the greater involvement of staff, cost control will also be better

- Budgeting and responsibility accounting implies providing **management control information**. This feedback system compares the performance and effectiveness of operating, with the plan. It also provides the opportunity for reappraisal and adjustment of plans.

- Budgeting helps to **determine priorities**. Management information produced by the budgeting process makes the complicated matter of running a business a lot easier. We are not just looking for a means of explaining variances; we need a flexible system, a guide, not a straitjacket. Given information, better decision making is possible as well as effective monitoring of progress.

- Budgeting is concerned with **Management Effectiveness**. It is better to do the right job moderately well than to do the wrong job superlatively well. Of course, it is better still to do the right job superlatively well!

2.2 Profit planning

Profit planning aims to set a profit objective for a budgeting period. Also, to establish the main policy decisions on how to achieve the objectives. The profit objective will normally be related to the 'return' required on the investment in the business. Profit planning evaluates alternatives to select the most likely to give the required profit objective. Managers can plan their budgets on this basis.

2.2.1 Purpose

The main purposes of profit planning are to:

- set profit objectives for the budget period
- state the policy decisions, and the course of action to be followed during the budget period
- give planning directives for preparing detailed operating plans.

The profit objectives will reflect the expected return on capital employed. This will depend on:

- the commercial environment in the budget period
- projected sales of the company
- past profit record
- maintenance of liquidity.

2.2.2 Planning guidelines

The main factors which must be specified in planning guidelines include:

- changes needed in volume, price and cost
- availability of funds for investment
- capital expenditure proposals

- changes needed in the level of working capital
- limits on discretionary expenditure, e.g. Research and Development.

2.2.3 Return required on capital employed

After the capital employed has been determined, then specify the required rate of return. Criteria include:

- what return could we get from alternative forms of investment?
- what degree of risk is involved in the company's activities?
- are the owners influenced by considerations other than profit, e.g. environmental, ethical concerns?
- comparison with competitor's performance in the same industry sector
- company's immediate past record
- expected trading conditions for the period of the profit plan.

The end result of this process is a statement of the profit objective and how it is to be achieved. This statement is the starting point for budgeting.

2.2.4 Profit planning techniques

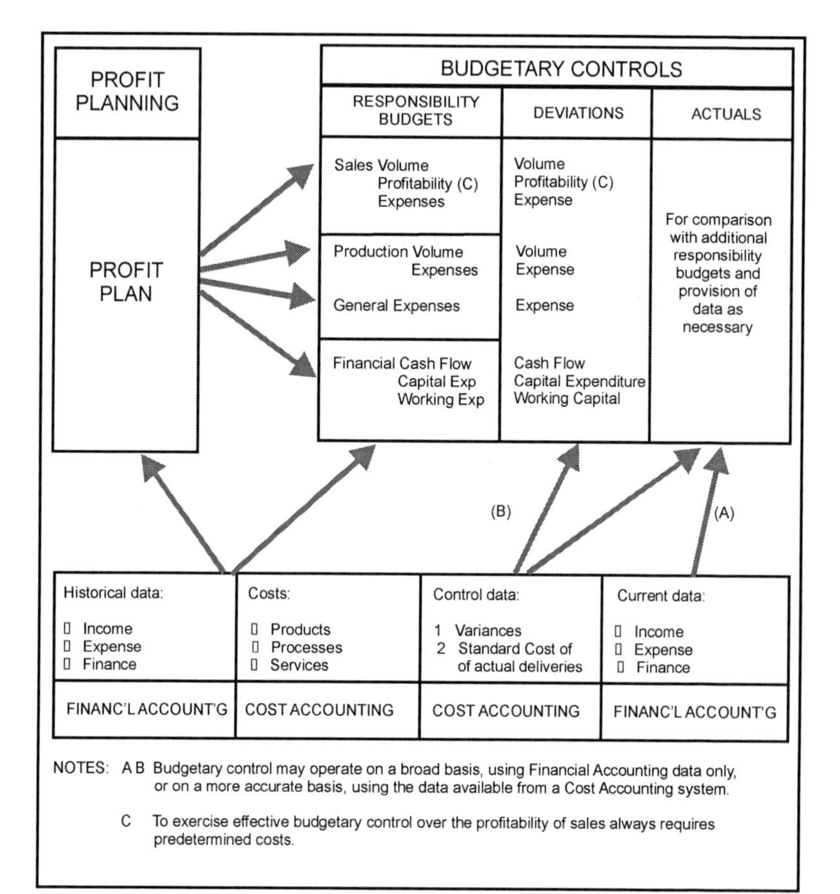

2.3 Types of budgets

2.3.1 Introduction

All managements make plans. A group of people not operating under some sort of plan is incoherent, directionless and not an organisation. In any organisation such as a company operating a business, the leaders (the managers), give much thought to what the objectives should be and the best way of reaching them. Although all managements plan, there are wide differences in the way in which they plan. Some people do their planning entirely in their heads. Others make notes and rough estimates on the backs of old envelopes! Still others express their plans in quantitative terms and commit these to paper in some orderly, systematic fashion. Some use computer models. However it is done, this process is called 'budgeting'. A budget is a plan expressed in quantitative terms.

Our concern is mainly with budgets that are expressed in monetary terms. Some budgets are expressed in units of product, number of employees, units of time, or other non-monetary quantities. As well as its planning function, the budget is also a control and co-ordination mechanism.

The diagram below illustrates the range of budgets that are possible, as well as the distinctions between the operating and responsibility budgets. As individuals we are mostly concerned with the latter.

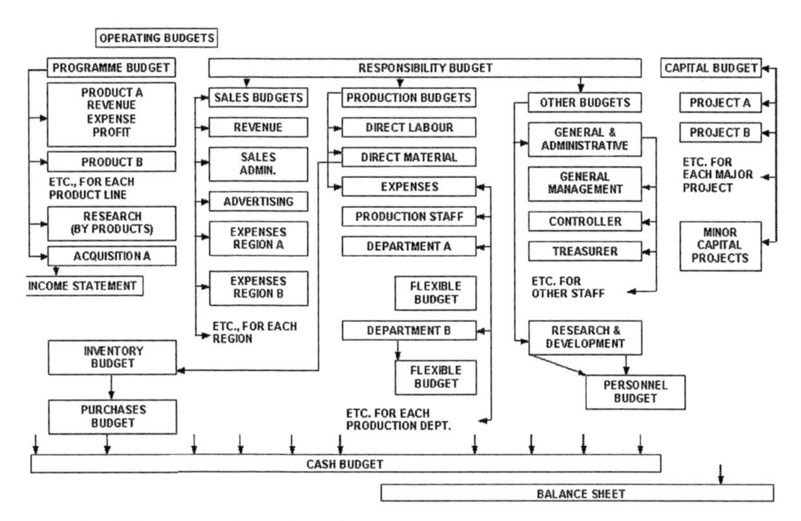

2.3.2 The sales budget

In any company, the most difficult estimate to make is the sales revenue. To do this, combine:

- a statistical forecast analysing general business conditions, market conditions, product growth curves, and the like, and

- an internal forecast, by collecting the opinions of executives and salesmen. (This will tend to be optimistic!) But it is always wise to involve salesmen in the estimating process.

There are advantages and weaknesses in these methods. Neither can be guaranteed to give an even reasonably close estimate; the future is inevitably uncertain.

The sales budget is not a forecast. Forecasts are important but passive; a budget reflects the positive actions that must be taken in order to influence future events. For example, this may be the sales forecast:

'With the present amount of sales effort, we expect sales to run at about the same level as currently.'

This is vague and indeterminate. By contrast, the sales budget might show a substantial planned increase in sales, reflecting management's intention to add salesmen, increase advertising and sales promotion, or redesign the product.

The budget is usually prepared in quantities, product, work hours, etc., then translated into money values.

Common headings are:

Products: Estimates need to be prepared for sales of each product in the range.

Territories: Sales of each product, by quantities and value, to be sold in each area.

Type of Customer: Important if different types receive special discounts, or special rates.

Salesmen: Sales by each seller, or agent, in a territory.

Month: To enable control checks of actuals/budgets.

Because it is information which greatly interests competitors, the sales estimate may or may not be given as part of the budget guidelines. Distribution may be restricted and summarised, with enough information to permit necessary planning.

2.3.3 The operating budget

The operating budget has two parts: a 'programme' budget and a 'responsibility' budget. Both arrive at the same figure for projected net income and return on investment.

i. The programme budget

This describes the major programmes that the company plans to undertake. This budget is arranged by product line and shows the anticipated revenue and costs associated with each product. This type of budget helps to answer questions such as:

- Is the profit margin on each product line satisfactory?
- Is production capacity sufficient to support the sales organisation?
- What can we afford to spend for research?
- Are adequate funds available?

If we get negative answers to any of these questions, the plan needs revising.

ii. The responsibility budget

This sets out budget information by responsibility areas. It is thus a control device – a statement of standard performance against which actual performance can be compared.

The costs in a responsibility centre will vary with volume. The responsibility budget shows the expected costs at various volume levels.

Also there will be responsibility budgets for a variety of other special purposes.

2.3.4 The capital budget

The capital budget is prepared separately from the operating budget and lists projects for the acquisition of new assets. Each proposal needs justification. A lump sum is often included in the capital budget for projects that are not large enough to warrant individual consideration.

Capital budget projects will generally be classified under the following headings:

- new asset acquisition
- cost reduction and replacement
- expansion of existing product lines
- new products
- health and safety
- legal requirements
- others.

Approval of capital projects in principle does not mean authority to proceed. Some worthwhile projects may not be approved because funds are not available.

Follow-ups on capital expenditures include checks on the spending itself and comparison of how near the estimates of cost and returns were to actual. If there are wide variances, then a revised capital budget may be necessary to provide additional resource appropriation.

2.3.5 Other budgets

i. Project budgets

Projects are long term and may stretch over several annual budget periods. The term 'project' is used to indicate, for example, the construction of a building rather than a one off major purchase, normally covered in the capital budget.

Long-term project budgeting has many difficulties, among them cost escalation and design changes. No project will go exactly according to plan. Flexibility and possible re-planning have to be built in to the project budgeting process. The project budget is essentially a control mechanism to give early warning of cost and time overruns.

ii. Manpower budgeting

Manpower is the most expensive and complex resource in any business. In a responsibility accounting system, each cost centre manager will specify the people resources available and required to carry out this section of the operation.

Employment costs need careful consideration. These are affected by internal factors – promotions, bonus, pay rates, overtime etc., and external factors – inflation, taxation and social security costs. Plans to increase or decrease manpower will reflect these factors. Compiling a manpower budget in detail allows the manager to make the fullest use of existing resources and, by reorganisation when necessary, improve productivity.

iii. Revenue and cash budgets

Revenue budgets are primarily concerned with Sales Income or income generated in other ways. Revenue needs to be scheduled as to when it is expected to come in and how it is to be allocated. This is part of the function of the Cash Budget.

The operating budget is prepared in terms of revenues and expenses. For financial planning purposes it translates into cash receipts and cash disbursements. This is the cash budget. Cash budgets ensure that the company has enough, but not too much, cash on hand during the period ahead.

Preparation of a cash budget

- Calculate and project forward cash receipts and cash disbursement items.

Remember:

- Exclude depreciation and other non cash items from the cash budget.
- Round-up figures. This is normal in budgets. The users of the

budget do not need precise estimates. Rounded-up whole numbers are adequate.

iv. Discretionary budgets

A discretionary budget is an unspecified lump sum which states what it is for, what the maximum sum overall is to be, and possibly specifies also a maximum sum per item.

Discretionary budgeting is useful in situations where expenditure for each item is of small value. The administrative cost of dealing with each item far outweighs the control benefit available. But control is maintained within the lump sum budget.

2.4 The budget as an operating plan

2.4.1 Purpose

In budgeting, every member of management should become involved in the financial planning and control process.

Budgeting may be described as:

- **Establishing requirements and objectives for all accountable managers.**

- **Preparation by each accountable Manager of a detailed operating plan for the department.** (This will meet, or improve upon, the departmental objective.)

- **Consolidation of all operating plans into a master budget.**

- **Reconciliation of the result with the profit objective.**

Budgeting is a creative part of the management process. So include a review of operating at each stage in the budgeting process. The review ensures that the operating plan represents the optimum use of resources.

The ultimate responsibility for the budget is the accountable manager's. High standards in setting operating plans develop cost and profit conscious attitudes in the whole management team. This makes effective use of the budgeting process.

i. People skills

The budgeting process should be perceived as a means of expanding job interest and increasing people's value to the company. This needs great skill in dealing with people by senior managers and the accounting staff who generally administer budgets. They have to know the management team, and the personalities involved and be aware of the different approaches which best suit individuals.

ii. Create the right conditions

There must be a mechanism (e.g. budget coordinator) to provide the linkage between all sections of the management team and their information sources.

Create conditions where management has the competence, and the will to work towards the achievement of their own and the company's objectives. These conditions include:

- top management commitment
- delegation through a management structure
- accountability for planning and control
- training.

iii. End result

The end result of this effort is an operational budget for the company for the period of the plan. It includes the master profit plan which shows the profit objectives. The subsidiary budgets include:

- department income and revenue budgets
- production costs budget
- budgets for current and fixed assets
- cash budget.

Each of these subsidiary budgets contains financial targets for individual managers. These are the plans prepared by the manager for the department.

The operating plan of itself will not lead to profits; managing to the operating plan will help to achieve the profit objective contained in the plan.

2.5 The budget as a control mechanism

i. Principles

Budgetary control is using the budget as a standard for measuring performance. Taking action indicated by this information is the main purpose. The key word is: ACTION.

There are four main functions, in a continuous action cycle:

- measurement and reporting of actual performance
- comparison of actual performance with budget
- planning the action required
- taking action.

ii. Measurement and reporting of actual performance

For budgetary control to be effective, it must be based on records of actual performance which are:

- accurate.
- readily comparable with budget.
- accepted by managers as resulting from their decisions.
- timely.

➢ **Accuracy**

Input to a control system comes from information supplied by staff. Departmental managers must ensure that the figures meet the required standard of accuracy. If they are not, important decisions may be taken on the basis of doubtful information.

- **Comparability**

  The budgeting system should exactly follow the pattern of the reporting system.

  Managers are committed to manage their activities within their budgets. Responsibility for deciding on the form and content of control statements is that of the line managers using the statements. The purpose of control statements is to enable them to measure their achievement. Therefore, set up the form and content of statements which will be most useful for comparison of budget with actual performance.

  The principle of 'Exception Reporting' highlights important items, and excludes trivial matters.

- **Acceptability**

  Comparison statements need to be acceptable.

  - Only charge expenses against a manager's budget if he or she has authorised the charge.
  - Accounting procedures must be able to verify charges against budget as correct and authorised.
  - Produce reports on a scheduled frequency which encourages action to be taken.

- **Timeliness**

  Reports must be produced on a timescale which permits realistic action if it is needed.

iii. Comparison of actual performance with budget

Comparison of actual and standard performance for any department is done by variance analysis of deviations by cause and by responsibility. Variance analysis should be used at the level which provides real information which will trigger action.

iv. Planning and taking the action required

Evaluating deviations and planning action should be a regular procedure. Formal action meetings should be held at which details of agreed actions are recorded for follow-up.

Any proposed action may require amendment of budgets, or a supplementary budget:

- to provide a revised measurement standard for how effectively the action is carried out
- to ensure that any action does not adversely affect other company activities.

If action is not planned (and taken) to correct an adverse deviation, reduction in planned profit is implicitly accepted.

The purpose of control is to enable managers to act to achieve planned performance. If there is an adverse deviation, nothing will be achieved until there is action to correct it, or to minimise its effect.

To sum up:

➔ Responsibility Accounting is a basic part of good budgeting; budgets should be prepared by the people who will be responsible for achieving them.

➔ Budgeting is concerned with management effectiveness – doing the right job, right.

➔ Profit planning aims to set the profit objectives for the budget period, and will determine the guidelines for compiling the budget.

➔ There are various types of budget. Distinguish between operational and responsibility budgets. The sales budget is the most difficult to compile accurately. Capital budgets deal with asset acquisition. All budgets need to be expressed in money terms.

➔ The budget should represent an operating plan and a control mechanism for achieving the plan.

3

Budget Control Systems

3.1 Setting up the control system

3.1.1 Steps required

It is not possible to carry out the budgeting process without the formal delegation pattern contained in an organisation structure.

i. Define organisation structure

If the organisation does not have a formal structure, one must be set up. This will define:

- limits of financial responsibility
- profit and cost items for which each Manager is responsible.

ii. Establish budget centres

These are activities for which separate budgets will be prepared. They are derived from:

- areas of responsibility as shown in the organisation structure
- natural divisions of the company.

iii. Establish cost centres

Cost centres are subdivisions of each budget centre. A separate analysis of expected outgoings is needed for each cost centre. For example, if the budget centre is a transport pool, the cost centres could be groups of, or single vehicles within the pool.

iv. Establish unit of cost for each cost centre

It is necessary to establish an appropriate unit of cost for each cost centre. If there is only one product, the unit will be the physical unit of the product, e.g. pieces, lbs., tons, kilos, etc. If different products use different amounts of the cost centres facilities, the cost unit has to be a unit of input such as in the case of the transport pool, something like cost per kilometre or cost per ton per kilometre.

v. Establish cost definitions

The definitions for the costing system must be established. This means that:

- the areas for which costs are needed have to be identified
- the exact nature of the costs required is specified for each area
- the appropriate cost information is defined.

vi. Material prices

The best method for setting material prices is standard costs. The responsibility for providing prices on this basis has to be agreed.

vii. Establish usage standards for products

Usage standards for materials, labour and machine time are required for all products to establish:

- budget of costs for physical units
- manning figures for labour budgets
- budgets of raw materials.

Establishing realistic usage standards requires that:

- responsibility for providing standards is defined
- responsibility for authorising changes in standard is defined
- procedures are in place to inform all departments concerned about standards, and of authorised changes in standards.

viii. Establish costs for service industries

This is more tricky. However, the major cost, labour, can be readily calculated. There will generally be some material cost, even if it is only stationery, some machine costs such as computer usage etc. It may be possible to set standard costs; more often educated guesswork will be used for budget estimates.

ix. Establish capital budgeting procedures

Capital budgeting is an important part of the budgeting process. It is necessary to set up procedures for initiation, evaluation and authorisation of individual projects. Authorisations need to be consolidated into an overall capital budget.

3.2 Budgeting and financial control

3.2.1 The control mechanism

Budgetary control compares the budget estimates of revenues and expenditures with the actual revenue received and expenditure incurred. All budgets including the working capital and cash budgets have this essential control aspect.

The budget as a control device, works through reports, plus meetings to discuss the reports. Reports are compiled to show the budgets, actual revenue and/or expenditure, the variance between actual and budget, and usually, the percentage variance. If the comparisons show 'significant' variations, comment as to causes is included, to assist in taking action.

i. Report contents and usage

Reports highlight 'significant' budget deviations and possibilities for improvement. They should show:

- what costs should have been (i.e. what has been budgeted)
- how close we are to meeting these costs
- whether performance is improving
- the variances – knowing the causes will help in their reduction.

Reports go to different levels and types of responsibility in the organisation. Each level of reporting is inter-related; reports at one level are analysed in greater detail at the next level. Effective reports relate to the responsibility of in a single individual or team.

The table below shows an example of reports received, and the information provided at operational and management levels.

LEVEL	SALES MONTHLY	MARKETING COSTS MONTHLY	ROAD TRANSPORT MONTHLY
	Budget vs actual and analysis of variances	Budget vs actual	Standard vs actual cost analysis of variances
Managing Director	by product groups for company	Total costs by major cost headings	Total
Marketing Director	by product groups for (a) own customers (b) Sales Manager's customers	Costs by major cost headings (a) controlled personally (b) controlled by Sales Manager	by vehicle group
Sales Manager	by product groups for (a) own customers (b) Export Manager's markets (c) sales reps' markets	Costs within his control analysed by subordinates	
Export Manager	by product group and geographical market		
Sales Representatives	by individual products and, if appropriate, customers		
Distribution Manager			by individual vehicle plus analysis of cost variances
Operations Manager			costs and variances within his control by individual vehicle
Maintenance Supervisor			costs and variances within his control by individual vehicle

REPORTS RECEIVED – LEVELS AND INFORMATION

ii. Reporting levels

Reports to top management are designed to show the overall performance of the organisation compared with budget. They indicate departments or functions which need attention. The trend in the performance of the organisation can also be indicated. The contents of the reports should be simple and limited to data on which action can be taken.

Regular meetings, review reports and actions taken.

The 'exception principle' means systematic appraisal of variances. Check that all non-controllable variances are outside the firm's control.

Be familiar with the controls operating within the firm whether they are accounting ones, or standard costing or budgets.

iii. Types of control comparison

Budget vs Forecasting	How are we doing? Are we on track towards our objectives? Will we remain on track towards our objectives? What will happen if no action is taken? Do we need to take action?
Budget vs Revised Forecast	Will the proposed action put us back on track?
Latest forecast vs Previous Forecast	Why has the forecast changed? Is the situation improving/deteriorating?Did things turn out as expected? If not, why not? Are we being too optimistic/pessimistic in our forecasting?

iv. Significant variances

It is impossible to budget with absolute accuracy. Variances at different levels arise randomly from period to period. Interpretation of variances must take into consideration whether or not a particular variance is 'significant'. For some types of costs, each budget period can be taken in isolation; judgment on whether the budget variance is 'significant' can be made without reference to variances of previous periods. With this type of cost, the variances of one period do not necessarily influence the variances of subsequent periods. Trends of past variances may enable a 'significant' variance to be anticipated.

For many costs, the budget will represent the average period cost expected over the whole year. Variances from the budget will arise randomly from month to month. For example, 'repairs and maintenance' costs may be budgeted on the same basis from period to period, but the costs will be uneven during the year. Adverse and favourable budget variances will occur randomly from period to period, but will offset each other over the year. The cumulative variance will not be 'significant'.

We need to determine whether a budget variance in a particular period is simply an expected random deviation, or a 'significant' deviation from the budget. Examine the cumulative budget variance to decide whether it is 'significant'.

A variance will be 'significant' if it is so big that it is unlikely to have arisen by chance. But calculation of budget variances does not necessarily reveal whether the variance is statistically 'significant'. Some variations from budget are inevitable and attributable to chance. Other important larger variations have controllable causes. These must be traced and action taken immediately they become known.

The principal indications of 'significant' variances are:

- the variance is outside the control limits
- several variances, especially if consecutive, occur near the control limit
- an undue number of variances are above or below the budget
- an increasing adverse or favourable trend shows in the variances.

v. Variance control charts

Variance control charts can be used to show the control limits and actual budget variances. These enable both significant variances to be isolated and possible future 'significant' variances to be anticipated.

Different control limits may be established for different costs. For example: in absolute terms, a 3% variance from budgeted cost of £100,000 is more critical than a 10% variance from a budgeted cost of £1,000. The absolute as well as the percentage variance must be considered when establishing control limits.

The following diagram illustrates the 'normal' variance limits tolerated for the cost centre, 'repairs and maintenance'. Within a 5% variance no investigation is required. Above the 5% limit a watch must be kept; above the 15% limit an immediate investigation is triggered. If the graph line consistently remains above or below the budget line, then the overall annual variance will form the basis for next year's budgeting estimates.

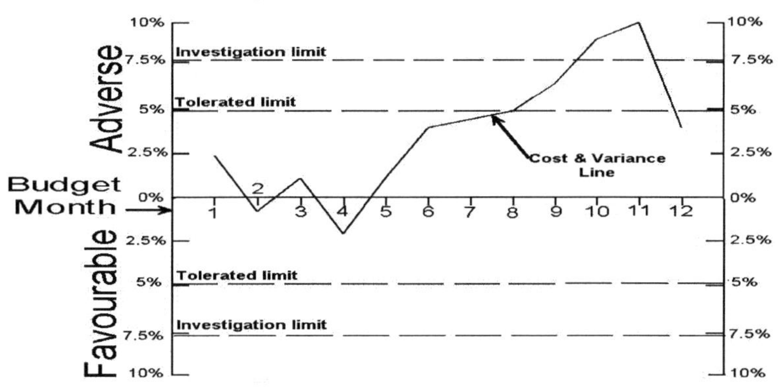

vi. Overhead variances

An overhead variance is the difference between the manufacturing overhead incurred during a period, and the standard overhead, charged to production during that period. This variance has three general causes:

- **Overhead cost variance**. The overhead budgeted for actual capacity is determined from a flexible budget. If actual overhead is more or less than the amount that should have been incurred for the actual production, there will be an overhead cost variance.

- **Volume variance.** The volume variance is the difference between the standard cost and the flexible budget for actual hours production. If actual production is less than normal capacity an unfavourable volume variance arises.

- **Overhead efficiency variance**. This is the actual hours needed to produce the actual production, being greater or less than the standard hours specified.

The three variances are illustrated below:

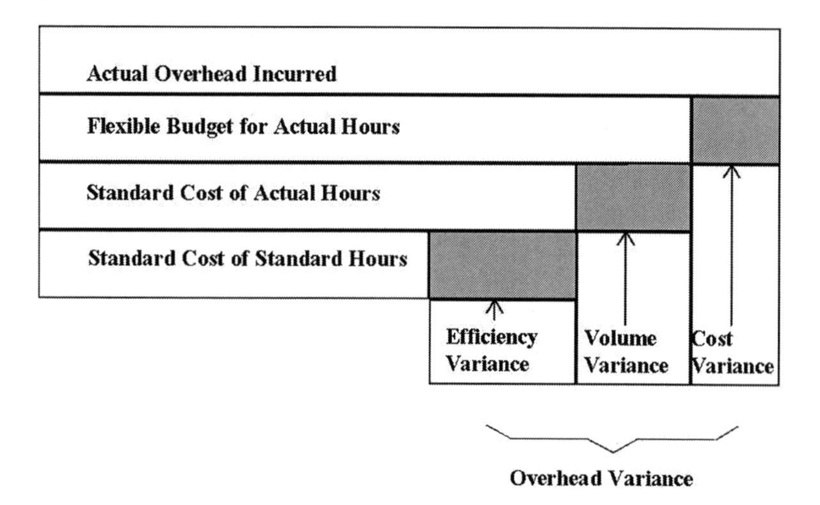

It is important to recognise that the overhead variance arises from one of the three causes described. This will assist in taking action to correct the variances.

vii. Developments in budgetary planning and control system

In recent years, sophisticated budgetary planning and control systems have been developed. These are based on the need to anticipate future sales, costs and cash flows in a dynamic environment. Traditional budgetary planning and control systems are of limited value for this purpose. We also have to consider human behaviour. Budgetary planning and control systems are designed to help people to manage and control their own work and that of others.

Two major influences can be identified:

- First: computers, quantitative techniques and more refined accounting procedures have led to an 'information revolution'.

- Second: a rapid expansion in organisational theory, to gain new and more realistic insights into human behaviour in organisations.

viii. The impact of the information revolution

Computers have enabled the development of sophisticated budgetary planning and control software which facilitates forecasting and budgeting with ease and speed. Nowadays, manually operated budgetary planning and control systems cannot meet the requirement for rapid access to relevant information.

Budgetary modelling has strengthened both planning and control. At the planning stage, budgetary models look across departments and responsibility centres and allow effective allocation of resources. The necessity of an accurate and up to date reporting network/organisation chart is emphasised.

Planning budgets flow from these computer-based models, and translate into control budgets with responsibilities clearly defined by individuals. The sensitivity of the budget to changes in key variables before and during the planning period can also be tested. This enables us to ask and obtain answers to 'what if' type questions; for example:

What if ... wage rates increase by 15 percent from Period 5 onwards?

What if ... the price of raw material X increases by £5 per ton in Period 7?

What if ... we fall short by 10 percent in our sales budget?

What is ... the impact of varying rates of inflation on working capital and cash flow?

If key variables do change, budgets and profit plans can be updated quickly.

A computerised budgetary planning model can:

- shorten the planning cycle by removing most manual calculation
- improve accuracy of budgets
- have continuous rolling budgets, made possible by speed of calculations
- use spot analysis by questioning results and examining assumptions on input data
- evaluate alternatives by asking 'what if' type questions
- educate, by bringing into open view data and computational procedures which allow us to question each other's assumptions and decisions.

At the budgetary control stage, computer models can determine the impact of reported variances. It is important to report exceptions, indicating whether they are 'random' or 'significant' deviations from budget. If it is 'significant', what will its effect be in the future? Some models report not only variances for the past period, but also the variances that are to be expected in the following period unless action is taken.

Concentration on selective attention directing reports, backed up by an on request reporting facility is possible. There can thus be reduced emphasis on routine reporting.

Developments of this nature allow us to concentrate on determining 'information needs'. This means discussion and thinking about what information we need to input into the system, to generate user-useful and attention-directing reports.

3.3 Flexible variable cost budgeting

3.3.1 Flexible budgets and overheads

Computerisation enables a flexible budget process to be implemented with comparative ease. The inputs can be manoeuvred to provide a flexible budget which is a series of static budgets designed to change in relation to the level of activity. Some costs vary proportionately with changes in the level of activity; others are semi-variable or fixed in nature. A flexible budget recognises the difference between fixed, variable and semi-variable costs.

Overheads include both fixed or period costs and variable costs. To control overheads, comparison of actual costs with budgeted costs for each cost centre is needed. The actual cost is compared with budgeted cost for the actual level of activity. The budgeted cost is derived from a fixed or static budget or from a flexible budget.

An overheads budget is developed for a specific estimated level of activity and specific operating conditions. It is designed to remain unchanged whatever the level of activity. But operating conditions and levels of activity normally vary from month to month. A fixed budget does not provide a fair allowance for overheads for any one month. It is unlikely that monthly variations will average out, so frequent revision of a fixed budget is necessary to make it a useful control tool. This is time-consuming and costly; so the flexible budget is more satisfactory and widely used. A flexible budget will show the true behaviour of the various items of cost in relation to changes in volume.

The key to the difference between a fixed and flexible budget is cost performance. This is measured by the difference between actual cost and the cost budgeted for actual activity. To get a clear picture of cost performance, compare actual cost at actual activity with budgeted (expected) cost at actual activity.

An example of a flexible budget follows overleaf.

A.B. & CO. LTD. FLEXIBLE BUDGET - SELLING COSTS. YEAR ENDING DECEMBER 31ST, 200X

Functional Cost	Fixed Variable Semi-Variable	Fixed Element	Variable Element per Std. Unit	Possible Sales Volumes (in $000's) and Related Costs					
				$600	$620	$640	$660	$680	$700
Variable & Semi-Variable Costs		$		$	$	$	$	$	$
Salesmen's Salaries	S.V.	14,000	1% on sales			20,400	20,600		
Salesmen's Commissions	V.		2% on sales			12,800	13,200		
Salesmen's Telephones	S.V.	200	½% on sales			3,400	3,500		
Salesmen's Travelling	S.V.	3,500	1% on sales			9,900	10,100		
Salesmen's Stationery	V.		¼% on sales			1,600	1,650		
Salesmen's Postage	V.		¼% on sales			1,600	1,650		
Bad Debts	V.		½% on sales			3,200	3,300		
						52,900	54,000		
Fixed Costs			Source of Information:						
Sales Admin. Salaries	F.	8,000	No. of employees			8,000	8,000		
Rent of Sales Office	F.	10,000	Contract			10,000	10,000		
Rent of Show Rooms	F.	5,000	Contract			5,000	5,000		
Depreciation of Equipment	F.	2,000	5% on Capital Values			2,000	2,000		
Insurance	F.	1,500	Insurance Policy			1,500	1,500		
Administration Costs - Sales Office	F.	1,000	Estimate Past Records			1,000	1,000		
Advertising	F.	12,000	Contract Ad. Agency			12,000	12,000		
						$92,400	$93,500		
			Standard Selling Cost per $100 of Sales			$144375	$14166		

To sum up:

➔ The budget is the control system as well as the operating plan for managing a business.

➔ Budgeting is the preparation of a detailed operating plan which will meet or improve upon the profit objective by providing control.

➔ The control mechanism works through reports on the various aspects of the activity of the business.

➔ Reports are directed to the various management levels of the business. They provide information on progress but, most importantly, give indicators for ACTION needed and to be taken.

➔ Reporting relies on variance analysis for its effectiveness. A variance (the difference between budget and actual performance) indicates that something is not going according to plan. Analysing the variance points the way to action.

➔ Budgeting systems have become very sophisticated with the advance of computer technology, which has made complex procedures simple and fast.

4

Specific Budgeting Items Considered

4.1 Revenue or income budgets

The main difficulty in compiling revenue budgets is the unpredictability of the income. Good forecasting is vital in order to establish a realistic level of expected income. Examine trends; analyse results and use statistical analysis in a sensible way to set income figures at a realistic level. Budgeted income levels are often the results of wishful thinking on the part of management.

Income has to be earned; first examine the existing corporate conditions and the resources which can potentially produce the income. Ask:

- Do we have the production capability?
- Do we have the qualified staff?
- Do we have the right plant?
- Do we have good marketing?
- Above all, do we have the financial resources to support the level of activity needed to generate the budgeted income?

If there are any negative answers, then the budget needs careful revision before even starting to put the figures together.

There is also the vital question: when does the money come in? Past experience will have established a pattern of payment; this may continue, but factor in possible variations. For example, if a large increase to the volume of sales is planned, it will be necessary to forecast a payment pattern from potential new customers, or a different market segment, of which we have little experience.

Income budgets work best on flexible budgeting principles. This gives the opportunity for rapid revision on a rolling basis throughout the year. Expense budgeting needs to be flexible so as to maintain firm control.

4.2 Expenses and costs

4.2.1 Limiting factors

The first step to establish is whether sales or production is a limiting factor. A limiting factor is where a resource – machinery, manpower or even money is limited in availability and will therefore restrict activity in some way. Thus if you have a shortage of skilled mechanics, production will be limited to what they can produce. Prepare a volume budget for the limiting factor. The rest of the budget is then prepared, taking agreed budgeted changes into account.

Review the standards to be used in the build up of costs and budgets. Decide changes to be made in standards, if any. These need to be included in the new operating plan.

Calculate a production budget for each cost centre. The budgeted output in physical units comes from this production budget. Convert this figure to money for each cost centre.

The following apply mainly to manufacturing businesses. However, similar principles operate for service businesses, in this case materials will be of little importance. But labour and overheads will become significant budget items.

4.2.2 Materials budget

This is derived from:

- budget volume of production
- standard material prices
- usage, waste and scrap factors.

4.2.3 Labour budgets

These are derived from:

- budget volume of production
- rates paid, including overtime, shift allowances and incentive payments
- usage factor from performance standards
- operating efficiency factors. e.g. labour performance
- grades of labour.

4.2.4 Overhead expense budget

This is derived from:

- budget volume of production
- budget volume of sales
- usage factors
- manning schedules
- related costs, e.g. charges on labour, social security costs etc.
- policy decisions, e.g. advertising, welfare expenses etc.
- company expense scales, e.g. for travel expenses etc.
- other factors, e.g. rental charges; other fixed costs, etc.

Some departments will have direct expenses, e.g. distribution may have a budget for carriage outwards.

4.2.5 Costs

Expenditure to be included in compiling a budget is broadly in two classifications:

- variable, and
- fixed.

Fixed expenditure is generally non-controllable. The amount is known and payable, whether the business is operating or not. Variable costs are controllable to a greater or lesser extent. Spend/no spend decisions are possible in most cases; also the level of expenditure is a matter for management decision.

The value of detailed budgeting is two-fold.

- It encourages greater attention to be paid to what costs are actually likely to be.
- It provides the essential element – the measure – in the cost control process, as well as providing the standard of performance.

4.2.6 Variable costs
These are developed by calculating two key factors:

- cost rates per unit of output (for each class of resources), and
- estimates of the volume of work to be done (in the period).

Obtain unit costs by considering all aspects of the activity:

- work method
- labour requirement and pay rates
- material requirement and costs
- plant usage and hire rates.

Standard costs, where available, may be used for budgeting.

Variances from budget will appear in the management report for the period in which the expenditure occurred. The variance may be within acceptable limits or, if not, must be explained and action taken to correct the variance, if possible. Labour and other variable cost budgets should be managed in this detailed way.

4.2.7 Fixed and semi-variable costs
The expenditure in this budget element is usually a known quantity, established either from historical data or from statements of future needs, at known prices. Salaries, rents, office equipment hire, telephone rentals are examples of fixed costs. They may change, but the change is known well in advance and these costs are not subject to variation in output. Some semi-variable costs such as printing and stationery, phone calls and so on, may for convenience be included

with fixed costs. These are items where fairly accurate forecasts of usage can be made. Cost, in these cases, varies with usage.

In preparing a budget, make a detailed analysis of the type of cost incurred in expenditure. This analysis will:

- separate fixed, variable and semi-variable costs
- examine plans and needs, especially in respect of variable costs
- ensure realisation that much forecasting is intelligent guesswork, and so make these estimates as fact supported as possible
- ensure acceptance of standards to meet
- make all concerned with the expenditure of money become conscious of getting value for money and good performance.

4.2.8 Standard costing

Standard costing is a technique of predetermining costs, by analysing all the cost elements included in an item. These are added together and taken as the norm cost for pricing calculations and budgeting. The actual cost of the elements included may, in operation, turn out to differ from the standard; this variance between standard and actual is the basis of budgetary control.

It is important to find the reasons for the variances and to put them right, thus controlling the costs. Consistent variations should lead to adjustments of the standard, to ensure more relevant control.

4.3 Capital budgeting

4.3.1 Long-range planning

An important part of the long-range planning process is the preparation of a capital expenditure forecast. The projects contained in the forecast will eventually appear in the annual capital expenditure budget. Initially the various projects have to be appraised in detail and submitted for approval. But capital investment appraisal techniques form only one part of the capital budgeting procedure.

The component parts of capital budgeting are:

- ✓ a creative search for investment opportunities
- ✓ long-range plans and projections for the company's future development
- ✓ a short-range budget of availability of funds and capital demanded
- ✓ a correct yardstick of economic worth
- ✓ realistic estimation of the economic worth of individual projects
- ✓ standards for screening investment proposals that are geared to the company's economic circumstances
- ✓ expenditure controls of capital outlays, by comparison of authorisations and expenditures
- ✓ candid and economically realistic post-completion audits of project earnings
- ✓ investment analysis of facilities that are candidates for disposal
- ✓ forms and procedures to ensure smooth working of the system.

4.3.2 Evaluating capital investments

Evaluation of capital investment decisions raises different problems from the measurement of past performance. In reviewing past performance of a business, the concept of return on investment (ROI) is the appropriate measure. Various profitability ratios are also used. However, this concept of measuring past performance ignores several matters which need to be taken into account in assessing future investments.

The basic object of any investment is that in return for paying out a given amount of cash today, a larger amount will be received back over a period of time. This larger amount should not only repay the original outlay, but also provide a minimum annual rate of return on the outlay. To obtain a true picture of the investment, all cash outlays and inflows must be taken into account. Also the value of a cash payment or receipt must be related to the time when the transfer takes place. It must be recognised that £1 received today is worth more than £1 receivable at some future date, because £1 received today could earn in the intervening period; this is the *time value of money* concept, the Discounted Cash Flow (DCF)/Net Present Value (NPV) method of project appraisal.

4.3.3 Required returns

Having calculated the rate of return for a project, it must then be decided whether the project is financially acceptable. Also what rate of interest should be used to discount the future cash flows of the project. There are three factors to be considered.

1. Cost of capital

The minimum acceptable return from any project is the rate of interest which the company is paying for the capital invested in the firm, i.e. its cost of capital. The objective should be to develop a financing structure which minimises the firm's cost of capital. As a standard part of its long-term financial planning and capital budgeting procedure, a company should regularly review its future financing programme.

2. Opportunity cost

All projects must compete with the return that the company could earn by investing its available finance outside the business. The risk and uncertainty attached to outside investments must also be taken into account.

3. Alternative projects

Where the company is in a capital-rationing situation, alternative projects will have to be ranked. These will compete with each other for the limited supply of finance available. Projects may be ranked by DCF rate of return.

4.3.4 Capital rationing and ranking

Some examples of ranking of Capital Investment proposals at a required rate of return are shown below.

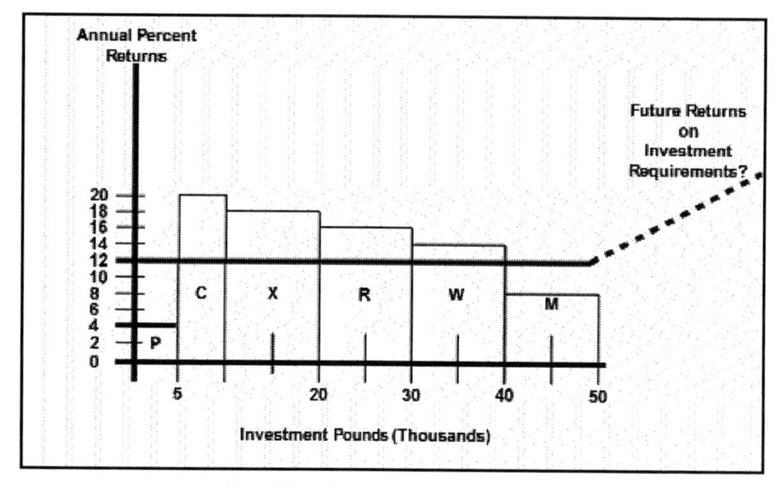

Ranking investment proposals

The diagram shows the ranking of the various proposals on the basis that a 12% rate of return is required and £50,000 is available. Project P is legally required, so ranks first. C, X, R and W are ranked in order of the estimated return. Project M fails to qualify; £10,000 of cash may be available for a more profitable project.

Examples of Capital Investment Proposals

Proposing Department	Cost/Estimated Return	Purpose of Investment	Description of capital need
R. Sales	10k – 16%	Business expansion	Growing market, one salesman added. To provide a car for his use.
M. Parts	10k – 10%	Replacement	Business expected to continue at same level. Storage racks in the Parts area are inefficient in design and layout.

W. Rentals	10k – 14%	New line	A new specialised line recently added. Have items available for short term rental.
C. General Office	5k – 20%	Efficiency	Accounting and billing work is substantial. New computer and software to make the office more efficient.
X. Engineering	10k – 18%	Expanded	Addition of a specialised capability machine to make mechanics more productive.
P. Special Projects	5k – 4%	Pollution control	Ministry of the Environment has demanded that special equipment be installed to stop pollution.

4.3.5 Capital project analysis techniques

There are five basic approaches to capital investment proposal assessment: Payback, Accounting Rate of Return, Net Present Value, Discounted Payback and Internal Rate of Return.

i. Payback

The payback method calculates the length of time taken by the project's net cash inflows to equal (and hence 'payback') the initial investment. If the payback period is less than that demanded for this type of project, then the project is acceptable. Payback is quick and easy to calculate.

ii. Accounting Rate of Return (ARR)

In this method, the accounting rate of return of a project is calculated as net profit percentage on capital employed after charging depreciation. The accounting rate of return can be determined for each year of the project, but is usually calculated as an average over the life of the project.

The accounting rate of return is readily understood and can be compared with accounting measures of performance.

iii. Net Present Value (NPV)

The NPV technique converts future cash sums into their present day cash equivalents. The method assumes indifference to receiving the present day cash equivalent ('present value') or the future cash sum at the future date.

For example: if you can lend and borrow money at 12 per cent per annum, then you should be equally happy to receive £100 now or £112 in one year's time. If you want to spend £100 now, either alternative would make that possible. The cash sum of £100 could be spent immediately; if £112 were to be received in one year, you could simply borrow the required £100 now. The loan and interest would total £112 at the end of the year and could then be repaid using the £112 receipt. All future cash sums can be similarly converted into their present value equivalents using present value factors.

iv. Discounted payback

It is also possible to combine the concepts of present value and payback to produce a measure known as the 'Discounted Payback Period'. Cash flows are discounted before accumulating them to obtain the payback period. The discounted payback approach takes into account when some of the cash flows arise and thus is somewhat more precise than the normal payback method.

v. Internal Rate of Return (IRR)

The IRR is the discount rate which produces a net present value of zero. It is the 'break even' discount rate and shows the maximum value that the cost of capital can reach before the project becomes unacceptable. There is no direct way of calculating the IRR; either a computer program is used or various discount rates are tried until a discount rate that produces a net present value of zero is found.

4.3.6 Project appraisal

These five methods of investment appraisal can give conflicting results; care is needed when using them. Of the five methods, only the NPV technique takes account of both the size and timing of all future cash flows. It is thus the only one of the methods to indicate by how much the economic worth of the business will increase as a result of accepting a project.

The payback period gives an indication of how long the project will require finance and, hence, what demands the project will make on the liquidity of the business. The accounting rate of return provides some guidance as to the likely future effect of the project on the return on capital employed. IRR indicates the maximum value that the cost of capital can reach before the project becomes unacceptable.

It is not usual to calculate all five measures. However, the NPV method does indicate the best long-term investment, but short-term considerations may mean that the payback period and the accounting rate of return have some influence.

4.4 Balance sheet budgets

4.4.1 Fixed assets budget

This budget should contain details of all expenditure authorised for fixed assets. The budget should distinguish between the date of purchase or completion and the date of payment.

4.4.2 Working capital budget

The main items in a working capital budget are stocks, debtors and creditors. Budgets for these items should be on a period by period basis. There are two steps in working capital budgeting:

i) Establish budget levels in relation to sales. For each item, a budget level for a given level of sales should be determined. For stock this will depend on factors which will be particular to the business. They include, for example:

Raw Material
- number of different items
- reliability of suppliers
- standard or special product
- proximity to suppliers
- value of stock

Work in Progress
- length of production cycle
- number of different items
- value of stock

Finished Goods
- commercial policy, e.g. same day delivery
- number of items

For debtors, the proportion of debtors to sales depends on:
- terms of trading
- effectiveness of credit control.

For creditors, the relevant relationship is to purchases. The proportion depends mainly on terms of trading.

ii) Relate these proportions to the budgeted level of sales and purchases for each period.

4.4.3 Cash Budget

This is the final budget. It is derived mainly from the profit plan, the working capital budget and the fixed capital budget. Other items which are included are taxation, dividend payments and capital amounts to be received or paid.

The purpose of the cash budget is to ensure that the operating plan can be carried out within the limits of available finance. The cash budget should be prepared for each accounting period, so that any peak requirements can be ascertained, and any shortfalls signalled and provided for.

To sum up:

➔ It is very difficult to predict income precisely accurately. But try to get as realistic a figure as possible using all available information.

➔ Be aware of the limiting factors in the operation of the business; good budgeting will depend on getting the balance right.

➔ The value of detailed budgeting is two fold.

- It encourages greater attention to be paid to what costs are actually likely to be.

- It provides the essential element – the measure – in the cost control process, as well as providing the standard of performance.

➔ Expenses are made up of fixed, variable and semi-variable costs. Standard costing can be used to calculate budget expenses in many areas.

➔ Separate budgets need to be prepared for any proposed capital expenditure. There are various techniques for evaluating capital expenditure proposals.

5

Forecasting

5.1 Introduction

Forecasting is the projection of past events to see how they might influence future events. We try to ascertain what is most likely to happen, given certain assumptions. It is a vital part of budgetary activity. Many elements of a budget require that we attempt to predict the future. Such predictions cannot just be pulled out of the air with any hope of being realistic.

Clear objectives cannot be established unless a systematic attempt has been made to foresee the future. Forecasting sales or expenses is NOT writing a budget; budgets are formulated as a result of the forecasting and then become a commitment.

5.2 Forecast periods

Long-term forecast

This will generally be for a period more than 10 years ahead. It is speculative in nature and will not be accurate. It can, however, predict certain trends.

Long-term operational forecast

This will be for a period of 5-10 years ahead. Objectives having been firmly established, this period is the longest required to realise those objectives. For example: a power station will take 5 years to build and commission. The forecast for electricity consumption must, therefore, be based on a minimum period of 5 years ahead.

Immediate forecast

This is about the short term, the year ahead. It is the forecast which forms the basis for establishing the immediate objectives of the business – turnover, profit, sales targets by products, markets, territories and so on. This forecast also forms the basis for planning, management and control of day to day operations, and the foundation for the company's budget.

5.3 Rolling forecasts

Many organisations use a system of computer-aided rolling forecasts – the horizon of the budget is rolled forward each quarter or half year. In this way, the organisation always plans at least a year ahead.

It is possible, as this exercise takes place, to analyse very recent variances. Also to forecast short-term future variances. This will enable management to take action before problems arise.

The budgetary control system is a powerful management tool. But the degree of detail of the forward projections inevitably becomes less precise towards the end of the rolling budget period. For example, the first three months will be budgeted in detail, the second quarter in less detail, and the final half in outline only.

Rolling forecasts need top management commitment, especially in the early development, until the procedures become well established. They can be time-consuming and put individual managers under pressure. However, the benefits of better management control outweigh these problems, once systems are established.

5.4 Why targets are vital

Any company must have soundly based planning to control its rate of growth and to relate its revenue and profits to the market return on investment.

In terms of sales, a company should never get into a position where it is:

- ✘ selling more products than it can provide
- ✘ selling less products than production has planned to produce
- ✘ selling a 'product mix' which is out of line with the optimum manufacturing mix
- ✘ selling a product or mix of products which is out of line with the market.

The company must set sales objectives. They should be:

- ✓ **quantitative** – the objectives should be amounts of money, or numbers of units

- ✓ **measurable –** so that monitoring of performance can be set against budget and indicate variances

- ✓ **specific** – each salesperson must know what his or her own objectives are and to which period they relate

- ✓ **attainable** – too high and sales people are demotivated – too low and they fail to produce their full potential

- ✓ **related to incentives** – if the company operates an incentive scheme

- ✓ **accountable** – if people are given an arbitrary set of targets to meet for the next year, there is a good chance they will ignore them. Each manager must estimate the potential overhead for his area, discuss with his superior and finally agree on the targets that he will accept. He will then be accountable for achieving those targets.

The following table illustrates who is involved, and what factors affect the forecasting process.

FORECASTS	FACTORS WHICH AFFECT THE FORECASTS
Salesmen estimate sales.	Increased orders from new and existing future customers. Effect of competition on sales (+ or -).
Sales supervisor adjusts estimates	Sales force potential. Increase in number of salesmen New selling methods Training
Branch regional manager adjusts figures	Local economic factors and market trends Competitors/Share of market Promotions
Sales director makes his adjustments and renegotiates any changes with his managers	Sales policy and budgets New products Market development Total market potential Market share. growth rate Advertising and promotion
Board of Directors makes final decision	Company's overall policies Strategic objectives Tactical plans Cash flow Return on investment Resources Company growth Share prices

5.5 What sort of targets

Here are three typical statements in terms of sales – cases of 'think of a number and double it'

- 'I reckon I can increase this year's figures by 20%.'
- 'I think I might manage an additional 5%.'
- 'Surely, you don't think we're going to get increased business with the sort of recession I've got in my area?'

There is only one way to prepare a meaningful forecast – that is, properly! Detail, detail and more detail! It is not a job that can be done in a few hours. Two or three weeks or possibly months may be nearer the mark.

Increased business can only come from two areas:

- more business from existing customers
- business from new customers.

The base line from which to work is a continuous breakdown of current and past business from existing customers. Deal with each grade of account in turn, starting with Grade A (very good) down to Grade C, or even D (poor prospect). Consider what increase (or decrease) in the sales volume is realistic.

Then, analyse estimated business.

✓ Itemise in detail all probable (and attainable) business from existing customers.
✓ Get an indication of order quantity/value for next year. Ask the customer.
✓ If the customer cannot supply the information, then make an educated guess from past history. Remember the competitors.
✓ New business. With no records available, estimates have to be made. Estimates can be based on factors such as grade of prospect, type of business, competitors' activities, etc.

Forecasting is not an exact science. However, interpret historical data correctly, and project forward realistically and the 'lucky guess' element is considerably reduced.

5.6 Factors to consider in forecasting

There are many factors which can affect the future of the economy in general, and the individual business in particular. The forecaster must, therefore, identify which factors are likely to affect the business and the relative importance of each one.

The variety of factors which should be considered when making a forecast include:

Socio-economic factors

1. Population:
   - Births
   - Emigration
   - Marriages
   - Age distribution
   - Deaths
   - Geographic distribution
   - Immigration
   - Minorities
2. Employment and Income
3. Consumption and expenditure
4. Distribution of goods and services:
   - Retail
   - Wholesale
   - Import
   - Export
   - Transport
   - Communication
   - Geographical location
   - Prices
   - Finance
5. Production of goods and services:
   - Food and agriculture
   - Building and construction
   - Fuel and power
   - Raw materials
   - Industrial/intermediate materials
   - Finished goods and services
   - Geographical location
6. Technological innovations

7. Political changes
8. Climate/weather
9. Environmental considerations and legislation

Market factors

1. Products, processes or services and their applications
2. Consumers/users and their requirements
3. Prices and margins
4. Manufacturers/suppliers
5. Distributors/intermediaries
6. Export/import
7. Volume of business in money and quantities by:
   Products, processes or services
   Consumers/users
   Manufacturers/suppliers
   Distributors/intermediaries
   Export/import
8. Structure of the channels of distribution relationships between:
   Eventual consumers/users
   Manufacturers/suppliers
   Distributors/intermediaries, etc. and any significant changes that are taking place in this structure
9. Promotional efforts by manufacturers/suppliers, etc.
10. Developments of new products, processes or services.

Internal factors

The company's own human, material and financial resources.

5.7 Collection of information

Forecasting is like market and economic research; there should be a continuous, appropriate level research function in any business. All sources of relevant information should be investigated.

These will include:

- published information
  - Government reports and statistics
  - trade and technical press
  - trade and research associations journals
  - Chambers of Commerce reports
  - buyers' guides
  - bankers' and stockbrokers' publications
  - subscription services.

- unpublished information
  - external sources
    - ➢ trade and research associations
    - ➢ national associations (CBI, etc.)
    - ➢ Chambers of Commerce
  - internal sources
    - ➢ sales records
    - ➢ buying office
    - ➢ research and development.

Go back in history as far as it is intended to project forward. A 3-year forecast should be based on a minimum of 3 years' back data, longer if possible. Even for a one-year forecast, for budget purposes it is worthwhile to go back for at least two or three years for comparison of trends. Note any trends and changes which have upset past patterns. Then research the causes for those which are non-recurring, e.g. were the changes due to tax changes, strikes, severe winter, price increases, etc.? Do not project forward past data which includes the effects of non-recurring events. This will result in misleading forecasts.

5.8 Statistical methods of forecasting

There are several useful statistical methods which can improve the reliability of forecasting. Most are fairly complex and a good understanding of statistical analysis methodology is needed to use them successfully. Some of the methods are listed below:

Moving average

which provides rolling averages on which to base future demand patterns.

Exponential smoothing

where the latest data are given greater weight in constructing average tables thus emphasising the importance of recent effects on demand.

Logarithmic graphing

whereby graphs are constructed on log paper which enable the straight line effects to be projected forward.

Least squares

this is the technique of ‘scattering’ to ascertain potential demand.

Standard deviation calculations

to formulate a realistic variance for forecast data.

To sum up:

➔ **Forecasting is not crystal ball gazing. It is a vital precursor of the budgeting process and we need to base it as factually and soundly as possible.**

➔ **Forecasting can be done for any period, the longer ahead the less accurate. We are mainly concerned with the 'immediate' future, i.e. the budget year ahead.**

➔ **Targets are vital; good forecasting helps to set realistic and realisable budget targets.**

➔ **Good forecasting needs a lot of detailed work, fact supported, from a wide range of information sources.**

6

Administering the Budget Programme

6.1 Budget controller

Budgeting is a management function, not simply an accounting exercise. Thus support by top management is essential. It is a management responsibility to plan and control. The budgeting programme therefore needs to be well administered.

Primary responsibility for the administration of the budgeting programme is usually delegated to the budget controller, frequently an accountant. This is one reason why budgeting is seen as an accounting exercise. However, if it is to be effective, budgeting involves everyone in the business.

The budget controller's job is to co-ordinate and supervise all efforts to produce an effective budget.

The general duties of the budget controller include:

- ✓ coordinating the work of everyone involved in the preparation of the budgets
- ✓ preparing budget reports
- ✓ recommending courses of action that may be indicated by the budgets
- ✓ studying the budgetary planning and control system, to make improvements.

The budget controller has no line authority, except over his own staff. The development of the budgets is simply supervised and coordinated by him. Sometimes a budget task force is established; the members will be managers within each department directly concerned with the compilation of their budgets and ensuring that timetables and such like are met.

6.2 Who should participate?

The basic rule of budgetary control is that managers develop and accept responsibility for their own budgets. But the budgets should be the product of the efforts of all levels of management. It is essential that involvement in the budgeting process goes right down to shop floor level so as to get employee commitment and understanding. Managerial and employee involvement in the budgetary planning and control system is essential for its success.

> *'Our experience is that the best solutions can be frustrated unless they are implemented with management understanding, involvement and commitment. This was something which my company failed to fully recognise when we first introduced budgetary planning and control. Some managers saw the preparation of budgets as a meaningless chore and even a threat. In consequence, much time and energy were wasted in producing meaningless bits of paper.'*
>
> Lord Sieff
> Chairman, Marks & Spencer

6.3 Budget steering committee

6.3.1 Composition

In some companies, a budget steering committee is set up, composed of executives in charge of major functional areas of the business. This committee will work with the budget controller and is a top level means for coordinating and reviewing the budget programme, particularly in respect of general policies which affect the budgets. This committee is normally advisory; it has the following functions.

- ✓ Establish procedures and timetables for the development of budgets.
- ✓ Set up guidelines for the overall budget and individual areas as necessary. The guidelines, which the budget committee agree, govern the preparation of the budget. They can be either very brief and general; or extensive and detailed.
- ✓ Receive and review individual budgets.
- ✓ Suggest revisions.
- ✓ Decide general policies affecting the budgets of more than one department.
- ✓ Approve budgets and later revisions;
- ✓ Receive and consider budget reports showing actual results compared with the budget, and
- ✓ Recommend action where necessary.

The budget steering committee is an influential group in coordinating the activities of the firm, in developing corporate policy and interpreting the budget guidelines. The budget controller will work closely with the budget steering committee.

6.3.2 'Bottom up' or 'top down' approach?

There is no single structure or approach to a budget. In the 'bottom up' approach, the budget can be assembled from all departments. But if the organisation requires significant improvement in performance, the management may specify the level of performance they will accept. This will drive the process from the 'top down'. Managers must then determine how they will meet requirements. Most budgets will contain elements of both approaches. This ensures that budget performance meets management's expectations and does not reduce the roles of individual managers.

Whether the emphasis is 'top down' or 'bottom up', those preparing the budget must ensure that individual plans conform to the group or company approach, without significant deviations. In issuing budget guidelines, emphasise the key features of company objectives and strategy. For a group, common assumptions should be used where appropriate. For example: exchange rates, interest rates for each currency, inflation and national economic growth and market size. These assumptions may be made centrally, after conferring with the units concerned. Individual managers may need assistance with the assumptions, to ensure consistency.

All these issues should be summarised in a formal document which can be circulated to and agreed by all of the managers responsible. This is the budget manual. Planning meetings with all managers will also be necessary to ensure that they are fully involved and ready to take responsibility for their budgets.

6.4 Budget manual

The budget manual will contain:

- the objectives of the business
- the part which budgetary planning and control plays in the accomplishment of these objectives
- the specific procedures to be followed in the preparation of the budgets

- models of the forms to be used and instructions on completion
- the reports comparing budgeted and actual performance to be prepared
- the functions of the budget controller and budget committee, and their relationship with the various levels of management in the development of the system of budgetary control
- a glossary of terms and definitions.

6.5 Budget preparation and document flow

The budgetary planning and control system is made up of many individual budgets; these individual budgets are then integrated into a master budget. The following is essentially the procedure for a manufacturing situation. But it can be adapted for, say, a retail situation or a service industry.

The following steps develop the individual budgets and the master budget:

✓ Prepare a statement of the basic assumptions on which the individual budgets are to be based. These will include company objectives for profits, growth and financial position for the budget period.

✓ Prepare a forecast of the general economic situation; also conditions in the industry, and for the firm. The basic assumptions and the forecast should flow from the long-range plan.

✓ Prepare a sales budget based on the forecast and the productive capacity of the firm. The sales budget will be broken down into areas of responsibility, for example, by salesmen or area sales managers. The sales budget will determine how much is to be spent on marketing and distribution, and what quantity of goods are to be produced.

✓ Prepare a production budget based on, and in conjunction with, the sales budget, after making necessary adjustments for planned stock changes. It will also include planning the requirement for materials, labour and manufacturing facilities together with the costs of these items. The production budget will be subdivided into budgets for each production centre.

✓ Within each production or cost centre, prepare budgets for each area of responsibility, i.e. budgets for responsible departmental managers based on their authority.

✓ Prepare marketing and administrative expense budgets for each responsibility area.

✓ Prepare a research and development budget analysed into projects by responsible research staff.

✓ Where applicable, prepare profits budgets by areas of profit responsibility and by major product or activity groups.

✓ Prepare a capital expenditure budget covering all non-recurring expenditures on fixed assets.

✓ Prepare working capital budgets covering all changes in raw material stocks, work-in-progress, finished stocks, debtors and creditors.

✓ Prepare a cash budget reducing all activities into cash flows.

✓ Assemble and co-ordinate individual budgets into a master budget, that is budgeted profit and loss account and balance sheet. From the master budget the budgeted rate of return on capital employed can be calculated; management can decide whether it is an acceptable return for the budget period.

✓ If the master budget does not achieve management's objectives, amend the budget process until a fresh set of budgets based on alternative assumptions is prepared which gives a satisfactory result.

Budgeting must be based on realistic assumptions with the master budget representing achievable targets. A budget which is not thus based is less than useless, and may do positive damage to the firm's operations.

6.6 The basis for estimates and forecasts

The managers of the various cost centres have primary responsibility for the preparation of the budgets.

For example: the sales forecast should be developed by the department with responsibility for marketing; this may be the sales department or a particular department which specialises in market research or economics. The sales manager must actively participate in the development of the sales budget and be directly responsible for the achievement of the sales.

The organisation chart overleaf shows how the annual budgets of a marketing department are developed.

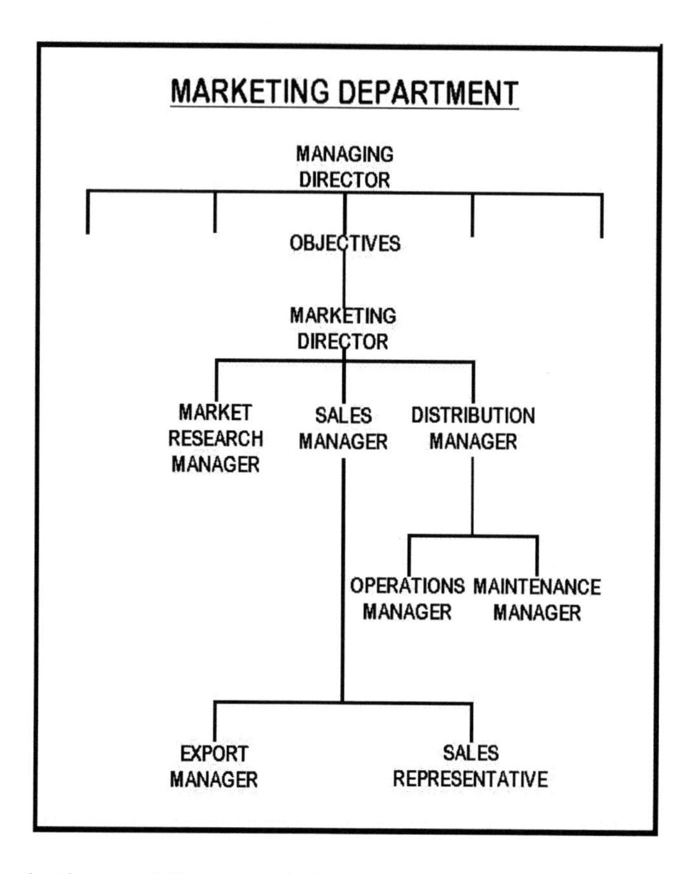

The budgeting workflow is as follows:

- Company objectives flow down from the managing director to the marketing director.
- The market research manager supplies marketing and customer research information to the marketing director and the sales manager.
- The marketing objectives and strategy to achieve the company objectives are developed by the marketing director and his senior staff and agreed with the managing director.

- The marketing objectives and strategy are translated by the marketing director into specific market-share objectives, geographic sales objectives by product groups, and class of customer.

- The marketing director passes to the sales manager objectives for all customers and geographical areas.

- The sales manager develops a budget for direct customers, and passes to the export sales manager, and the sales representatives objectives for their areas of responsibility.

- The budgets flow up the organisation for agreement by superiors, i.e. the sales representatives and export sales manager agree their budget with the sales manager, who in turn agrees the total sales budget.

- The agreed sales budget is passed to the distribution manager. It is also passed to the finance director, production director, and to the managing director.

- The budget for selling and marketing expenditure is developed in a similar manner.

- The sales budget forms the basis for the distribution manager to develop the budget for distribution and transport function. This is also agreed with the marketing director and passed to the accounting department.

- The sales, marketing expenses, and transport budgets are consolidated into the master budget by the budget controller for approval by the managing director. The managing director presents the master budget to the board of directors for approval.

Each manager and the staff of a responsibility centre participates in the development of their budget. This general procedure applies to every segment of the business equally.

If a departmental manager has been given objectives to accomplish on which there has been no agreement or consultation, there will be considerable demotivation. The opportunity for all levels of staff to participate in budget development is vital if realistic outcomes are to be achieved.

6.7 Revision and approval of budgets

The development of budgets at the departmental level does not imply that the budget must be fully accepted. It has to be agreed with the manager's superior and this will mean agreeing changes with the manager. It is usually the responsibility of the budget committee to review the departmental budgets and build them into a unified master budget. Adjustments will inevitably be required. If the budget committee makes alterations to departmental budgets, these should be negotiated with the departmental managers so that they feel they have participated in the review of their budgets.

To sum up:

➔ For successful budgeting a good administration system is essential. The more involvement in the process, by everyone, all down the line, the better the budget will be.

➔ The managers of the various cost centres have primary responsibility for the preparation of the budget.

➔ The budget controller is an individual who assumes responsibility for getting the budget together. There is often a budget steering committee also, who will have the final say in the revision and approval of the budget.

➔ Putting the budget together is usually a mixture of 'bottom up' effort and 'top down' direction. This ensures good guidance plus motivation and creativity which leads to commitment to achieve the budget objectives.

➔ The Budget Manual contains the procedures, processes and format for compiling the budget, as well as step by step guidance on the flow of documentation through to the completed budget.

7

Zero Base Budgeting

7.1 Introduction

Zero Base Budgeting (ZBB) is budgeting from scratch. It is a system where each function or programme in an organisation, whether new or old, must be justified in its entirety when a new budget is formulated. The method does not assume any increase over the previous period's budgetary base of expenditure, hence the term Zero Base.

7.1.1 What is Zero Base Budgeting?

ZBB is:

- ✓ a management process.
- ✓ a planning and budgeting process.
- ✓ a process which recognises budgeting as a key decision making process (whether decisions are made consciously or not).
- ✓ an analysis and decision making process – which results in a budget.

ZBB is not:

- ✗ conceptually new;
- ✗ a 'budgeting' process;
- ✗ 'reinventing the wheel'.

7.1.2. Why the traditional system fails

In the usual budgeting approach, expenditures approved in the current period's budget are often automatically accepted for inclusion in the next budget. Only increases are analysed and discussed. There is the implicit assumption that current programmes should continue; that the only way a new programme can get into the next period's budget is if new funds become available. Thus the existing situation continues.

Such Budgeting abuses are called 'ten percentism' or 'creeping incrementalism'. The budget for the current period is usually taken as read, needing little justification beyond that offered in the past. The procedure then is for departments to take the current year's budget and add ten percent (or such other appropriate rate to allow for inflation), and to make a specific allowance for any new commitments.

The ten percent is added in the full expectation that it will be reduced by 5 percent! The golden rule for the head of the department is 'ask for more than we received last time and spend all the funds each year'. Using up the funds is proof of need; the person who seeks economies and does not spend all that is available, is in danger of having the budget for the next period reduced. The net result is that, at best, the department receives more than it did last year and at worst, not less than it received last year.

This diagram illustrates the effect of creeping incrementalism. The budgets grow even larger. Value for money becomes questionable.

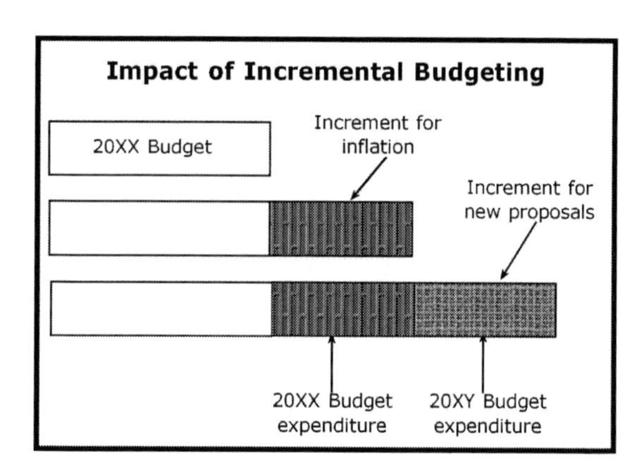

7.2 Steps in implementing ZBB

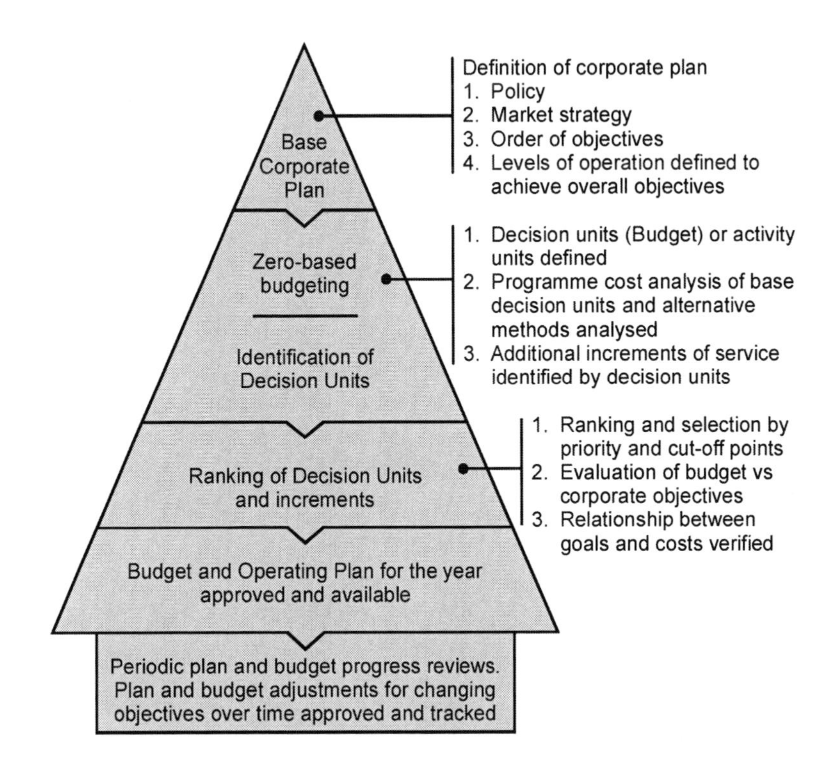

Steps in implementing ZBB (starting at the apex)

7.2.1 The corporate plan

ZBB must start with the corporate plan. If the budgeting process has not been integrated with the future corporate plan, then the process is worthless. To plan properly, such factors as corporate philosophy, goals, objectives, marketing strategy and levels of operation required to achieve objectives, must be defined prior to budgeting. The next step is to develop a budgeting process which will align all operating units with the corporate plan. The system must be designed to present alternative action plans, possible reductions, and necessary expansions.

Definition of corporate plan:

- policy
- market strategy
- order of objectives
- levels of operation defined to achieve overall objectives.

7.2.2 Identify 'decision units'

The decision unit may be the same as a department or cost centre. Or a Manager may wish to separate out different significant size functions that require separate analysis. Thus there could be more than one decision unit for any department.

ZBB focuses management's attention on evaluating activities and making decisions about their continuation. The 'meaningful elements' of each organisation must be determined so that they can be isolated for analysis and decision making. These meaningful elements are 'decision units'.

In practice, top management will define the divisional or departmental levels and then leave it to divisional/departmental heads to separate out decision units for separate analysis.

7.2.3 Describe each decision unit in a series of 'decision packages'

7.2.3 i The decision package concept

The decision package (operational plan) is a document which identifies and describes each decision unit in detail. Management can evaluate it, rank it against other decision packages competing for funds, and decide whether to approve the funding or not. The content and format of the decision package must provide management with the information it needs to evaluate each activity. The document must state:

- ✓ the goals of the decision unit;
- ✓ the programme by which the goals are to be achieved;
- ✓ the benefits expected from the programme;

- ✓ the consequences of not approving the package;
- ✓ the costs and the personnel the activity requires.

7.2.3 ii Alternatives

In developing the decision package, two alternatives must be evaluated:

a. Different methods of accomplishing the objective or performing the operation which are considered best. (e.g. in-house versus contracted maintenance services). If an alternative to the one currently being funded is chosen, the recommended one should be shown in the decision package. Note should be made that the current method was not selected.

b. Different levels of effort of performing the operation. A level of effort is the different commitment of resources to carry out the task at varying degrees of benefit to the organisation. Once the best method has been chosen from those being evaluated, a Manager must identify alternative levels of effort and funding to perform that operation. Managers must establish a minimum level of effort (which should be below the current level of operation), then identify additional levels or increments as separate decision packages. These increments may bring the operation up to and above its current level. Each level of effort identified will require a separate decision package.

Alternative levels of effort for the personnel function

Level of effort	Activities to be undertaken
1	Maintain an office for interviewing prospective employees
2	Interview prospective employees and make recommendations to employing departments
3	Level 2, plus maintain personnel files on development of staff within the organisation
4	Level 3, plus conduct personnel management courses within the organisation
5	Level 4, plus operate training activities for unskilled staff

Thus, if the current level of effort for this activity is 2 (shaded), then additional decision packages will be required for levels 1, 3, 4 and 5, which will indicate justification and benefits as well as costs expected.

7.2.3 iii The most difficult stages

The identification and evaluation of different levels of effort are the two most difficult stages of Zero Base analysis. But they are key elements of the process. If only one level of effort were analysed (probably reflecting the funding level required by the Manager), and the request from the Manager for funds exceeded the total funds available, management would have to choose between:

- funding the programme at the requested level, thus reducing profits
- eliminating the programme

- making an arbitrary reduction in the level of funding (which frequently happens in traditional budgeting) or
- starting the budgetary process again.

7.2.3 iv Decision package alternatives

A decision package can further be defined as 'one incremental level in a decision unit'. There may be several decision packages for each decision unit. It is these incremental levels that get ranked. By identifying a minimum level of effort, plus additional increments as separate decision packages, each Manager presents the following alternatives for top management's decision-making.

- Eliminate the operation (if no decision packages are approved).

- Reduce the level of funding (if only the minimum level decision package is approved).

- Maintain the same level of effort (if the minimum level, plus one or two incremental levels bring the operation from the minimum level up to the current level of operation, are approved). The current level of effort refers only to the level of output or performance, sometimes referred to as the 'maintenance level'. However, even at the current level of effort, managers can change their method of operation and make operating improvements, so that the current level of effort is maintained at reduced cost;

- Increase the level of funding and performance (if one or more increments above the current level are approved). The operating Manager responsible for the decision unit normally does the analysis of that unit, being the most knowledgeable person about its operation, and will be responsible for implementation. This analysis will be reviewed by higher management levels and the financial staff. The result of this review may be the modification or the reduction of selected decision packages.

At each incremental level the costs and benefits should be shown.

7.2.4 The ranking process

Top management has to decide how much it should spend and how to allocate it between the competing programmes. This is done by listing all the decision packages in order of decreasing benefit to the organisation. The benefits to be gained at each level of expenditure are identified; the consequences of not approving additional decision packages ranked below that expenditure level are studied.

The process

- Evaluate and rank all decision packages by cost/benefit analysis to develop the budget request and profit and loss statement.
- Rank and select by priority and cut-off points.
- Evaluate budget vs corporate objectives.
- Verify relationships between goals and costs.

With the decision packages ranked in order of priority, management can continually revise budgets by revising the cut-off level on any or all rankings. This will mean that some new high-priority programmes have been funded by eliminating or reducing lower-priority, on-going programmes rather than by reducing profits.

Following the ranking process, the budget and operating plan for the year will be approved and available.

There should be periodic budget progress reviews. Plan for budget adjustments to take account of changing objectives over time.

7.3 Problems and opportunities in introducing ZBB

For ZBB to work, managers must be convinced that there is something in it for them. They will be asked to devote time to learning the new system – plus much more time and effort in planning and budgeting for their activities under ZBB. But a reminder of the drawbacks of the traditional budgeting system with its arbitrary across-the-board cuts is sufficient to persuade most managers that the system is better than the traditional one.

ZBB enables effective managers to attract more funds; efficiency is rewarded. Managers welcome the opportunity to participate in the analysis and decision-making process. It also gives them an insight into the workings of other departments – by reference to the decision packages. The increased 'visibility' of the operations of all departments, as presented in their decision-making packages, will give managers a better understanding of, and sensitivity to, the problems of the other managers.

Some managers will oppose ZBB since it forces them to display their effectiveness and justify what they are doing. ZBB requires an adjustment of attitudes and perhaps a change in the management style of managers. These adjustments can be traumatic for some. However, if the continued viability of an organisation is at stake, even the most 'difficult' managers will probably be prepared to make the necessary adjustments and sacrifices.

7.4 Installing a ZBB system

7.4.1 Setting up a Task Force

A Task Force should be set up which will include operating and financial managers. They will design and administer ZBB. Operating people must be included; they are the most knowledgeable about operating needs and problems, and will mainly be responsible for implementing the system. Also they will add creditability to the proposed ZBB implementation plan.

The first job of the Task Force is to design the process to meet the specific needs and culture of the organisations. The basic concept of ZBB remains the same but the specific formats and implementation procedures will vary in each organisation.

The Task Force will have to prepare a simple budget manual that details the type of zero-base analysis required and explains the decision package and ranking concepts.

7.4.2 Benefits of ZBB

ZBB is an approach, not a fixed procedure or set of forms to be adopted uniformly from one organisation to the next. Nor is it an optimal answer to every manager's prayer for a simple, effective operational planning and budgeting system – but it comes close. ZBB forces managers to look at their corporate goals, objectives and strategies; then inform top management how much money is needed to attain them. This is done by focusing on the pounds needed for the programme's accomplishment, rather than on the percentage increase or decrease for the current year's budget.

ZBB enables companies to identify and compare priorities within and among different departments of the business. It allows a performance as promised, and shows whether duplications of effort exist. Budgets need not be recycled when expenditure levels change; instead, the decision package ranking identifies the operations which should be added or deleted to implement the budget change. As a bonus, ZBB gives everyone concerned in the process tremendous insights into the workings of the various departments and activities of the organisation.

To sum up:

➔ **Zero Base Budgeting is a management, planning and budgeting process. It is primarily used for the expenditure side of budgeting.**

➔ **Done well, ZBB can eliminate waste in expenditure budgets and create sound management effectiveness.**

➔ **ZBB depends on the same sort of management reporting structures as in the traditional system. However, ZBB looks at the responsibility areas in a more critical and detailed way.**

➔ **Expenditures need to be justified through a series of decision packages and ranked in order of priority, so that the resulting budget is flexible and gives good value for money.**

➔ **There are problems introducing ZBB, but also opportunities. Effective managers will attract more funds; it enables all management, from top to bottom, to look at their corporate goals with a clearer view. Everyone gets excellent insights into the whole activity of the business.**

8

The Company Budget

8.1 Introduction

Why budget? Are there any real advantages? To answer this question, analysis of business failures usually include reasons such as inadequate capital, excessive credit, overstocking and high costs of operation. All of these are symptoms of inadequate planning and lack of controls. Without planning, chaos is almost inevitable.

This chapter is essentially an extended checklist of what you already know from earlier chapters of this book. Use it to help set up your own budgeting process. Not all items will be relevant to your situation. Use what you need.

To develop a coherent and useful budget a business needs to have:

Objectives and a Plan

Objectives, statements of where the business is headed for, need a great deal of thinking about. Usually we will be able to state our objectives in financial terms: amount of sales and costs; usage of equipment; value of materials and their costs; employment of labour and their costs; and so on. Finally we arrive at a profit objective stated in money terms.

In order to achieve the objectives we need to have **plans** – how we are going to achieve our objectives. The budget is the statement of operational intent of the business. The budget document details, in a coordinated way, all aspects of the operation of the business, again stated in money terms.

8.1.1 Fundamental purpose of budgeting

The fundamental purpose of budgeting is to assist management to carry out its basic functions of planning, coordinating and controlling operations effectively. This is rather broad; more specifically, budgeting:

- ✓ forces serious thinking about basic policies
- ✓ requires proper organisation, and assignment of responsibility for each function of the business
- ✓ means that management, from the top down, must participate in the establishment of goals, and in making plans in harmony with other departments
- ✓ needs adequate historical accounting data, to put down in figures what is necessary for satisfactory results
- ✓ plans for the most economical use of resources
- ✓ helps remove uncertainty among lower levels of management about basic policies
- ✓ instils the habit of adequate consideration of all factors before reaching important decisions
- ✓ pinpoints efficiency, or its lack
- ✓ forces periodical self-analysis in the company and prompts understanding of co-workers' problems
- ✓ is the major check on progress, or lack of it, towards objectives.

Budgeting is not really a complex process. It is orderly planning of income, costs and capital expenditures for a period. It then compares what actually happened with the planned progress during the period; this gives indications of what corrective action or modification of plans is needed. This is budgetary control.

8.1.2 Other considerations

Budgeting must have the active support of top management. The best planned budget will fail unless it has this. Make sure that there is complete backing, and communicate this to the whole organisation. This will directly influence success.

There must be formal organisation and delegation of authority and related responsibility at all levels of operation. A budget is an efficient means of delegating authority and responsibility. Delegation of budgetary responsibility must be the same as operational responsibility.

Budgeting and accounting are clearly linked. In some businesses the administration of the budget will become a function of the accounting department. A separate individual, usually from the finance area, called the budget controller may be assigned to administer the budget.

Continuous budget education throughout the firm is absolutely essential. The uses and limitations of budgeting must be thoroughly understood by all.

Realistic goals must be established. Unrealistic goals, particularly when imposed from above, discourage and demotivate employees.

8.2 Preliminary checklist

Here are the steps that need to be followed in developing the budget:

- Review present financial statements, organisation charts and the chart of accounts

- The financial statements will provide comparative information on which to base projections of revenue and expenditure.

- Check that the chart of accounts is adequate for the analysis of expenditure needed.

- Look at the organisation chart critically. Does it represent the current responsibility and reporting structure accurately? Are any adjustments needed to reflect changes in the organisation?

- Determine what management reports will be needed

- Based on the organisation chart, plan what budget control information (reports) are needed, including the amount of detail and the distribution to each level of management responsibility.

- Appoint the Budget controller, who may be an accountant.

- Set up budget administration team.

- Set up a Budget Committee of a small number of senior managers, which may include the CEO.

- Establish assumptions and guidelines and publish these.

- Establish timetable and publish this.

- Draw up budgeting formats and distribute these.

- Get preliminary forecasting going.

- Start training sessions for budget preparation.

8.3 Types of budget

There are three principal classifications of budgets: the appropriation budget, the fixed budget, and the variable budget. The basic concepts concerning each of them are important.

Appropriation budget

This shows the amount of money which can be spent on a given item for the year. Advertising and research and development budgets are examples of appropriation budgets. The amount may or may not be directly related to the sales budget for the year; however, once an amount is established it will generally not change with sales volume.

Fixed budget

This is an unchanging plan. Once a level of activity is decided, the fixed budget is set at that one level. There are a number of disadvantages to the fixed budget; the major one is that cost of sales and operating expenses are predicated on one fixed volume of sales. If this sales volume is not realised or is exceeded, management has no real variance control based on the revised volume of sales. But many budgets are compiled on this basis and, because they rapidly become irrelevant, are ignored.

Variable budget

This is a refinement of the fixed budget; a series of fixed budgets. Variable budget construction involves analysing each expense account into its fixed, variable or semi-variable components. A formula by which each expense can be adjusted to the actual level of activity is developed.

Fixed costs are items such as rent and depreciations. Variable costs are those which vary proportionately with changes in planned activity, such as material and direct labour. Semi-variable costs are those which are composed of both fixed and variable elements. Semi-variable costs increase or decrease with various levels of activity; these changes will not necessarily be in direct proportion to activity.

Each expense item should be classified as fixed, variable, or semi-variable. This requires thought and sound judgment. Semi-variable expenses need to be separated into their fixed and variable components.

8.4 Active budgeting

8.4.1 Revenue (Sales) budget

The revenue budget is the heart of the system on which all else depends.

- ✓ Check forecasts for realism in current and future (1 – 2 years) economic circumstances.
- ✓ Check sales projections by relating them to past experience e.g. variance on budget/actual for past 2 years.
- ✓ Check capacity (production, warehousing, logistics etc.) to see if improved sales are feasible.
- ✓ Calculate profits in relation to expected sales. Is this an adequate return on investment?
- ✓ Make necessary revisions to sales budget.

8.4.2 Other budgets

Depending on the type of business there will be several other budgets to prepare. Among these will be:

Production budget

- ✓ Check level of stocks.
- ✓ Prepare materials forecast and budget, analysed by product.
- ✓ Prepare scheduled purchases budget; timed deliveries, quantities and payments.
- ✓ Prepare labour budget: staffing levels, pay rates and associated costs.
- ✓ Prepare manufacturing expenses budget to include all above and draft forecast Manufacturing Account.

Ensure that all these subsidiary budgets add up to the main budget.

Operating and administrative expense budgets

✓ Prepare budgets for all costs centres, e.g.:
- advertising and publicity
- communications (telephone, post etc.)
- distribution costs
- travel expenses
- maintenance costs
- research and development
- etc., etc.

These budgets will be prepared by the managers of the various departments and their staff, and integrated into the master budget.

Capital budget

✓ Check all capital asset registers
✓ List proposed new capital assets; date of purchase; depreciation schedule. These enter into cash budget calculations.
✓ Check DCF/NPV calculations

Cash budget

✓ Draw together all income sources and all cash outflows.
✓ Schedule these on a monthly basis to determine financing needs.

8.4.3 Drawing it all together

✓ Prepare budgeted financial statements:
- Manufacturing Account.
- Trading Account.
- Profit and Loss and Appropriation Account.
- Balance Sheet.

- ✓ Review these and the overall budget with senior management.
- ✓ Make agreed revisions and amendments to the budget.
- ✓ Review the applicable sections of the budget with departmental managers. Obtain agreement and
- ✓ Distribute final agreed budgets to all concerned.

8.4.4 Using the budget

- ✓ Develop period (usually monthly) reporting format and procedures.
- ✓ Review these reports regularly.
- ✓ Analyse variances and take action where appropriate and possible.
- ✓ Revise budget where necessary and recommend management action.

8.5 Selling, administrative expense and other budgets

All the various segments of the budget are important, but the budgets that will touch most people throughout the organisation are those covering selling and general administrative expenses. The budgeted amount allocated and agreed for these functions controls the work of many departments and is often the source of serious variations because of lack of skill or attention to detail by departmental managers.

The costs of getting the goods to market involve determining the fixed, variable and semi-variable elements of expense. Items such as commissions will vary directly with sales. Transportation expense will also vary directly with sales. Warehousing and storage vary with the level of inventory held. The budget should be prepared so that each sales manager is aware of the sales expenses for which he or she is responsible. Promotional expenses and travel may either be budgeted by the manager responsible for control of these expenses, or there may be a yearly appropriation budget based on the projected sales volume of the area.

Advertising is often treated as a separate budget. A definite amount is appropriated for advertising for the year; this budget is broken down by type of advertising media and by the month or quarter of expenditure.

Administrative expense should be classified by organisational responsibility. There may be divisions under the executive, the controller, and the treasurer. While many of the items in the administrative expense budget are fixed in nature, consideration should be given to the effect of sales plans or other activities on administrative costs. A change in sales policy, for example, which involves a change in distribution methods, may have a direct effect on costs. Each item will need to be analysed and a determination made as to the estimated cost.

Research and development expenses involve an intelligent assessment of an overall limit which the company can prudently spend on R & D. This should be based on both short- and long-term considerations and careful selection of projects on which amounts are to be expended.

The Capital expenditure budget will be affected by the plan to achieve projected production or service levels. It will also be influenced by the condition of the equipment and by the cost of maintenance in comparison to the costs of acquiring new equipment.

8.6 Income and expense statements and financial condition

The various detailed budgets having been completed, the cash forecast can now be prepared. This will include analysis of period financing needed. Following this, the income and expense budget is prepared.

This completes everything necessary to prepare a working trial balance, which is an accounting procedure to make sure that all the figures are correct. Insert the figures from the beginning balance sheet. To this, in an adjustment column, add the profit and loss items and cash receipts and disbursement items. These are extended to arrive at an ending balance sheet which is used for the statement of estimated financial condition.

8.7 Conclusion

The completed budget is reviewed by top management. Any necessary revisions are made. The sections of the revised budget are reviewed with the various levels of management responsible for carrying out the budget plan.

Distribute the budget, or applicable sections. Finalise the monthly reporting format, and procedures.

During the year, review monthly statements. Reasons for variances must be analysed and revisions to the budget made, where necessary. Management action to bring operations back to plan must be taken.

To sum up:

- ➔ This extended check list summarises the information about the reasons for budgeting, the procedures for getting a budget in place and using it.
- ➔ The budget is the statement of operational intent of the business; what is planned to be achieved and how it is to be done.
- ➔ The budget is also the premier control mechanism for ensuring that the business meets its objectives.
- ➔ There are different types of budget and different sections of the overall budget. These need to be brought together to form a coherent whole which governs the activity of the business.
- ➔ If it is to be used effectively, the budget, when finalised, must be an agreed statement by managers who will use it, and their committed intent to operate the plan fully.

Appendices

Having ploughed through the theory of budgeting, you might like to try a little hands-on experience!

Appendix 1

Acme Products Ltd gives a couple of typical examples of appropriation budgets. This is a type with which many people will be familiar. The formats given here are for the traditional budget setup. They are fairly simple and easy to understand and use. Forms can, of course, get much more complex and demand greater information, and can be completed as computer templates. But it is not simply a matter of filling in figures. A good deal of thought is needed: what has happened in the past? (we have some comparative figures for this); what is likely to happen in the future (the next year?). Do we need this level of activity? Will it increase/decrease? Should it? This needs a lot of thinking about and, if we are using ZBB principles, quite a lot of justification to decide any recommended changes.

It is worthwhile working through these examples to get a clearer idea of the budget compilation and calculation process.

Appendix 2

Cosmos Products is an example of working out and the research and thinking behind the calculation of a particular little budget segment. Again it would be a good idea to work through the examples to get a good grasp of how the figures are derived. However, to make it easy for you we have given a suggested answer. It will be beneficial to work through both the questions and the answer to get a good feel for how budget making works.

Appendix 3

This is a glossary of terms used in the text, which may be unfamiliar to some readers.

Appendix 1

Traditional budgeting formats and examples

These are completed examples of typical budget forms for representative cost centres for Acme Products Ltd. The Chart of Accounts and the Organisation Chart identify responsibility areas, for which expenses are incurred, and which are controlled by an individual. Within these cost centres, specific costs, as shown in the examples, are accumulated. In compiling the budget, it is important to look back and consider what has been spent in the recent past. This is shown in these examples. Current calculations are shown and the total compared to the past average to ensure that next year's estimate is reasonable. Remember, this is the traditional method.

If we use ZBB principles, we need to look at each expense item more closely to see whether the expenditure is still fulfilling its function, or is perhaps no longer needed at the budgeted level of activity.

The main point is that budgeting is a detailed process which needs attention from the person responsible for the cost centre, as well as all people concerned in working in the cost centre.

Here are two budget items of Acme Products Ltd., prepared for the Year 200Z.

Cost Item	Account No.	Budget Centre No.	Cost Centre No.	Budget Amount	Remarks
1	2	3	4	5	6
Travel & Entertainment	017	110	---	£ 60,000	See Schedule 1
Cleaning	032	136	---	51,400	See Schedule 2

Notes:

1 Name of Expense Centre
2 Chart of Accounts indicator
3 Budget (Responsibility) Centre identifier
4 Cost Centre – subdivision of the Budget Centre
5 Estimated Budget costs* Note that Travel is overestimated (Schedule 1) and Cleaning is underestimated (Schedule 2)
6 Explanation of Budget costs.

Budget Detail Sheet – Schedule 1a

TITLE: Travel and entertainment	Proposed by: ASM Approved by: SL	
Previous years	Actual cost £	% of sales
200U	20,100	1.0
200V	25,600	0.9
200W	30,200	1.1
200X	40,100	1.0
200Y	54,900	0.8
Budget estimate for 200Z	60,000	0.7

Budget Detail Sheet – Schedule 1b

Title: Sales Head Office	Details: Mileage claim by salesman & entertainment expenses to correlate with sales.		
Account: Travel Expenses 110	Proposed by: A.S.M. Approved by: S.L.	Budget Year 200Z	
A/C No: 017	Title: Travel & Entertainment		
Content: Travel expenses including fares; air fares; mileage claims; out-of-pocket expenses; entertaining customers and potential customers.	To Form No:	Date:	By:

	Previous Years						
	200U £	**200V £**	**200W £**	**200X £**	**200Y £**	**Total £**	**Average £**
Travel Expenses:							
Air Fares	4,500	6,000	6,200	6,500	12,500	35,700	7,140
Mileage claims by salesmen	9,000	11,000	13,000	18,000	24,000	75,000	15,000
Entertainment:							
Managing Director – potential clients	3,000	4,000	6,000	6,000	11,000	30,000	6,000
Sales Personnel – Manager & Salesmen	5,300	4,000	4,500	4,000	6,200	24,000	4,800
Out-of-pocket expenses	300	500	500	800	1,200	3,300	660
	22,100	25,500	30,200	35,300	54,900	168,000	33,600
No. of Air Travel p.m.	2	2.5	2.5	3.5	5.25		
No. of Salesmen	15	17	17	18	20		
No. of Customers with accounts larger than £50,000	20	25	28	30	32		
£10,000 - £50,000	30	40	45	50	60		
Mileage Rate	30p	35p	35p	40p	40p		

Budget Detail Sheet – Schedule 1c

<table>
<tr><td>BC</td><td>CC</td><td colspan="2" rowspan="2">Account</td><td colspan="3">Proposed by: A.S.K.</td><td rowspan="2">Budget Year
200Z</td></tr>
<tr><td></td><td></td><td colspan="3">Approved by: S.L.</td></tr>
<tr><td>No.</td><td>No.</td><td>No.</td><td>Title:</td><td>To Form No:</td><td>Date:</td><td>By:</td><td rowspan="3">Amount
£</td></tr>
<tr><td>110</td><td>--</td><td>017</td><td>Travel & Entertainment</td><td></td><td></td><td></td></tr>
<tr><td colspan="7">Budget for 200Z</td></tr>
<tr><td colspan="7">Travel expenses by M.D.
1 flight per week @ £200 — £200 x 52</td><td>10,400</td></tr>
<tr><td colspan="7">Mileage claims by Salesmen:
£100 per month per salesman — £100 x 20 x 12</td><td>24,000</td></tr>
<tr><td colspan="7">Entertainment:
M.D. - allow @ 0.15% of Sales : 0.015 x 8.57 million</td><td>12,800</td></tr>
<tr><td colspan="7">Sales personnel - 0.08% : 0.008 x 8.57 million</td><td>6,900</td></tr>
<tr><td colspan="7">Out-of-pocket expenses : 0.002 x 8.57 million</td><td>1,700</td></tr>
<tr><td colspan="7">Agreed Budget Total 200Z</td><td>55,800</td></tr>
</table>

Budget Detail Sheet – Schedule 2a

TITLE: **Cleaning**	**Proposed by: Building Maintenance Supervisor** **Approved by: C.A.**	
Previous Years	**Actual Cost £**	**% of Sales**
200U	16,100	0.8
200V	19,200	0.7
200W	24,200	0.9
200X	32,100	0.8
200Y	44,900	0.6
Budget estimate for 200Z	£51,400	0.6

Budget Detail Sheet – Schedule 2b

Title: Occupancy

Account: Cleaning 136		Proposed by: Building Maintenance Supervisor	Budget Year 200Z	
A/C No: 032		Approved by: C.A.		
	Title: Cleaning			
Content: Cleaning of factory floor, general office, and officers rooms. Includes wages of full-time cleaners and cleaning materials and tools and contractor's payment.		To Form No:	Date:	By:

	Previous Years						
	200U £	**200V £**	**200W £**	**200X £**	**200Y £**	**Total £**	**Average £**
Wages to cleaners	4,900	7,300	7,400	8,800	9,000	37,400	7,480
Cleaning materials	3,500	3,600	5,850	8,000	8,400	29,350	5,870
Cleaning tools	200	260	450	600	600	2,110	422
Contractors	7,500	8,040	10,500	14,700	26,000	66,740	13,348
	16,100	19,200	24,200	32,100	44,000	135,600	27,120
No. of cleaners	2	2	3	4	4		
Area cleaned by outside Contractor	7,500	7,500	8,750	10,500	14,400		
Cleaning materials per cleaner	1,600	1,900	1,950	2,005	2,100		
Cleaning tools per cleaner	100	130	150	150	150		

Budget Detail Sheet – Schedule 2c

BC	CC	Account		Proposed by: A.A.			Budget Year 200Z
				Approved by: C.A			
No.	No.	No.	Title:	To Form No:	Date:	By:	
136	--	032	Cleaning				Amount £
Budget for 200Z							
Wages:							
No. of Cleaners				6 x £200 x 13			15,600
Cleaning Materials:							
£2,100 per cleaner				6 x £2,100			12,600
Cleaning Tools:							
£150 per cleaner				6 x £150			900
Contractors							31,000
Agreed Budget Total 200Z							60,100

Appendix 2

Cosmos Products

Attached are a Budget Detail Sheet and the proposed budget for 200X of the Printing and Stationery Department of this Company.

The Company manufactures and trades in plastic household utensils. Competition has been getting stronger but the company has been holding its' own and last year was able to make a significant breakthrough into some new export markets.

The Directors' budget guidelines indicate that they expect a 30% increase in sales over the average of the last five years

Cosmos Products – Budget Detail Sheet 200X (Y/E 31.12.200X)

Administration Department

A/c No:	0-028
A/c Title:	Printing & Stationery Section
Section Head:	A.B.C.
Section function:	Provide printed internal stationery, reprographic and photocopying services. Printing of internal and publicly distributed brochures.
Budget Content:	Printed forms; paper; letterheads; brochures; general printing. EXCLUDES product promotion materials, general stationery supplies.

	Previous Years						
	200S Actual £	2000T Actual £	200U Actual £	200V Actual £	200W Actual & Estimated £	Total £	Average £
Printing							
Invoices	6,000	12,000	16,000	21,000	26,000	81,000	16,200
Letterheads	8,000	18,000	19,000	26,000	35,000	106,000	21,200
Account Forms	6,000	24,000	13,000	14,000	22,000	79,000	15,000
Brochures:							
Annual Accounts	10,000	12,000	14,000	16,000	18,000	70,000	14,000
General Supplies:							
Printing Supplies	4,100	9,500	11,200	12,900	17.600	55,300	11,100
General Supplies	16,100	26,900	17,400	32,200	46,100	138,700	27,300
	50,200	102,400	90,600	122,100	164,700	530,000	106,000
Sales £'000's	780	960	1,340	1,875	2,250		
No. of Customers on Record	500	800	1,200	2,200	3,000		
No. of Accounts, including subsidiary ledgers	3,000	4,000	4,500	5,200	6,000		
No. of Shareholders on Register	8,000	10,000	11,000	15,000	16,000		
No. of Staff	8	12	15	18	19		

Cosmos Products – Suggested Budget for 200X

		£
Invoice Sets		
No. of Customers on Record	3,000	
Expected increase	20%	
3,600 customers x 6 invoices per year x £250 (per 1,000 invoice sets)		5,400
Letterheads		
6,000 Accounts x 6 statements per year x £200 (per ream, 500 sheets.	Say 22 reams = 4,400	
Continuation	10 reams = 2,000	6,400
Statement Sets		
6,000 Accounts x 6 statements per year x £250 (per 1,000)		9,000
Annual Accounts		
20,000 copies x £4.50 per copy		90,000
General Supplies		
£600 per year per staff member : 600 x 20		12,000
Printing Supplies		
£4,300 per month : £4,300 x 12		51,600
Proposed Budget Total for 200X		174,400

Appendix 3
Glossary

Budgeting	Budgeting is the process of preparing an operating plan for the business. It is generally stated in money terms.
Budgetary control	The process of comparing the budget figures with the actual costs incurred or income received, to ascertain differences and take action to ensure that the plan (budget) is being carried out.
Chart of accounts	A named listing of all the various expenditures and incomes. This is categorised by type of activity and given an orderly sequence of numbers. This facilitates analysis for accounting and budgeting control purposes.
Corporate plan	An analysis of the strategic intentions of the business, expressed through the budget, and other statements of the objectives to be worked towards.
Cost centre	A locus of activity within the business. It is signified by a numerical sequence in the Chart of Accounts, into which all the costs associated with the activity are gathered. Generally the responsibility of an individual who will prepare the activity plan (budget) for that part of the business.
Capital Investment Appraisal	Various methods of calculating whether a particular project or capital acquisition will produce a satisfactory return.
Expenses	Expenses may be fixed, i.e. contractual, with the amount known in advance; variable, i.e. the amount may vary with usage; or semi-variable, i.e. with an element of fixed, or known cost plus associated variable costs.

Flexible Budgeting This is the creation of a series of static budgets which are designed to reflect changes in the level of activity.

Limiting Factor The element in a group of factors which preclude further expansion as the resource has reached the limit of its capability, i.e. if there is a limited amount of raw material then the number of units produced must be limited.

Objectives A well thought out statement of the intentions of the business as to its activity and achievements required. This serves as a beacon to direct the efforts of all concerned in the business.

Organisation Chart/ Responsibility Network Generally this is a diagram which indicates the various departments and operations of a business. The most familiar type is the 'family tree', which shows responsibility areas for specific activities and reporting lines for budget purposes. Businesses change structure; it is essential that the organisation chart be kept 'live' to illustrate the organisation structure of the business now.

Profit Planning Consideration of alternative lines of action to choose those most likely to give the required results. It is an essential part in developing the budgetary control system.

Responsibility Accounting The theory that the person responsible for the activity of an area, compiles their own budget, is committed to it and is accountable for achieving the agreed results in the area.

Revenue Or Income. Monies coming in to the business by way of sales or other sources such as interest or dividends. But not Capital inflows which do not form part of the profit calculations.

Return on Investment (R.O.I.)/ Return on Capital Employed (R.O.C.E.)	The amount of surplus income over expenditures (profit), calculated as a percentage of the total net investment in a business. This is the classic indicator of business performance.
Standard Costs	A calculated cost for items of production compile of raw material costs, plus labour costs, plus overhead costs per unit of production. Used for budgeting and quotation purposes. Convenient to use but requiring great skill for accurate calculation.
Variances (or Deviations)	The difference between actual income or expenditure and that budgeted. Variances indicate problems in areas of business activity and are the basis for budgetary controls.
Zero Base Budgeting	A process by which budgets are calculated without reference to prior years, i.e. starting from scratch. An important means of fundamentally analysing the operation of a business and in making improvements.